Memoir of Muriel Viscountess Lowther

Andrew Watson

Grosvenor House
Publishing Limited

This book is published by
Grosvenor House Publishing Ltd
Link House
140 The Broadway, Tolworth, Surrey, KT6 7HT.
www.grosvenorhousepublishing.co.uk

A CIP record for this book
is available from the British Library

ISBN 978-1-80381-527-5

SIR GEORGE FARRAR
BY MURIEL,
VISCOUNTESS LOWTHER

CHAPTER 1

My father, Sir George Farrar was born at Chatteris in 1859. I remember my grandmother, she lived to be over 80. She was a very formidable old lady when I knew her, with very small feet and beautiful hands. She lived in a house in Bedford with a garden at the back, in which grew a giant mulberry tree, where we used to gather mulberry leaves for our silkworms. My grandmother wore a white lace and black satin dress and hair was smoothed flat and parted in the middle. Her slippered feet rested on a footstool where she always sat in front of a roaring coal fire with hands folded in her lap. Occasionally she went out visiting in her brougham, drawn by a very sedate horse and an equally staid coachman. Otherwise she sat by the fire, with the lace curtains drawn across the windows. I never remember seeing the windows open, even in the summer. She had a system of communication with Wooding, her parlour maid, or the cook or the housemaid. She blew down a pipe attached to a mouthpiece which connected to the nether regions with her long suffering staff. Her one and only companion was a sleek Persian cat who sat on the cushion on the other side of the fire.

The stairs were very steep and went up and up until you arrived at the top floor. My grandmother was very fat and it took some time to reach her bedroom, where she slept in a huge featherbed.

Years and years ago when my grandmother was small and very slim she married my grandfather, Dr Farrar. Tall, dashing and far too inconsistent for my grandmother, he would leave his practice for a day's hunting without a backward glance at his patients who forgave him because they all loved him, but he did not take his profession very seriously. He must have loved my grandmother, but perhaps he did not take her very seriously either. But my grandmother was not the sort of person that anyone could treat lightly, even when she was young she must have had a will of iron and a very conventional outlook on life.

My great-great-grandfather, who at one time of his life was Mayor of Bedford, was highly respected by the citizens of the town and my grandmother's father, Sir John Howard, was equally respected and the founder of an engineering firm called Howard Bros. Bedford was full of Howard's and their relations. So my grandfather, Charles Farrar, not only married my grandmother, but all her Howard relations as well. They were great family people.

All this was too much for my grandfather and for that matter for the Howards, who thoroughly disapproved of my grandmother's choice. So, in the days when divorce was never mentioned, except with bated breath, my grandmother, with the full approval of all the Howard clan, divorced my grandfather. So one day my grandmother, surrounded by all the Howards, in their frock coats and top hats and her four small sons, in their Sunday suits, clustered around her skirts, stood on the steps of Bedford Town Hall, leading down to the river, and they saw my grandfather off. He walked down the steps, got into his rowing boat and rowed away down the river to the fen country where he spent the rest of his life.

My grandmother returned to the fold in Bedford to become the poor relations of her father, John and later, her brother, Sir Frederick and with their help she educated her four sons.

She was far too determined to allow even her brother Frederick to interfere with their upbringing and far too independent to allow anyone else to discipline them except herself.

It was a challenge she accepted and years later, when each of her sons, in their different ways, had made a success of their lives, she still managed to keep a firm hold over them. As an old lady she became the matriarch and, writing endless letters, in a straight up and down handwriting, without any variation in the thickness of the strokes, passing news from one son to the other, keeping in almost daily touch with their activities and receiving daily visits from all her Howard relations, from whom she gleaned all related information about family affairs or political news, all the everyday news of the town and its inhabitants. Nothing, however spicy, escaped her attention, all of which she passed on from one to the other. She was the general confidante, sweet and understanding, but underneath she was as independent and as tough as old boots.

Every Sunday she went to church with her brother, Frederick Howard, he in his frock coat and square top hat, she in her best black dress and satin bonnet with satin ribbons decorated with pale mauve violets. They met at the church door and he waited while she descended from her brougham, arranged her black satin skirts and together they sailed up the aisle to sit in the front row of pews.

Her brougham would be waiting and back she would be driven to Sunday lunch, roast beef and Yorkshire pudding and apple tart and a nice snooze in front of a roaring coal fire for the rest of the afternoon.

"I think," she wrote to my father in one of her weekly letters, "that I will correct my remarks as to your needing to be meek, because there is a hymn in my book I will never sing, because I do not believe it. 'The modest and meek the earth shall possess'. When this is given out, I let the other people sing it and I stand and reflect. So few modest and meek possess the earth, compared to the elbowing people who stand for nothing but getting on in the world. Ah well, perhaps the modest people have great possessions in the beautiful life beyond."

My grandmother could never have felt lonely and neglected like so many old people today, because she had made herself the centre, around which all her relations rotated, whether they liked it or not, it was incumbent on them all to visit her each week.

My mother, the only one of her three daughters-in-law who was quite impervious, would sweep into my grandmother's house, ask her to admire her latest dress from Paris, regale her with all the latest bits of racy news from London, mimic all her friends, till my grandmother shook with laughter, tell my grandmother about her grandchildren, plump up the cushion on her chair, stroke the house cat and leave with a gust of laughter before my grandmother could get her breath, leaving behind a scent of wild briar rose and a fleeting kiss on the end of my grandmother's nose. But her other three daughters-in-law, paying their routine duty visits were subjected to the full weight of my grandmother's authority.

"My dearest to George," she wrote to my mother when she was nearing the end of her life, "as one gets so near the end of life the world and life grows more beautiful. I so look forward to the summer day when I shall see you. I have been reading some of your older letters and as I read of the old early days of struggle with bad times, I realise, even when you were so very young, how strong you were in principle and in character and how there has never been a break in your love for me, no weak or broken place in the chain. And now I am old this is so sweet a memory to me. I always say to myself on Friday, 'Tomorrow I shall get a letter from him.' I have been reading the life of George Washington. He had so good a mother. She prayed for all her sons. I have loved you all so much, but I do not think I have prayed for you as much as I ought."

Whether she prayed for them or not, the fact remains that she brought up four sons virtually single-handed without any money and launched them all into a world of adventure, in which, in their own way, they all succeeded. The eldest son, Sidney, joined his uncle's firm and went to South Africa. Percy hated South Africa and later became president of the Alpine club and besides editing the Alpine Journal was an experienced climber and equipped the first expedition to Everest. Fred, as the youngest, became Headmaster of Elstow school and Dean of Bedford. And there was my father.

When he was 16 my father left school and went to work in an office in London. At school he had always managed to pass all his exams by cramming, but otherwise my grandmother said his work was deplorable. He had to account to my grandmother for every penny he spent, so he wrote everything down in a small cashbook which he carried about in his pocket. On the Saturday, if he had anything left over to spend, he would beg or borrow something for a day's hunting and he saved up his money to buy breeches and boots.

Sir John [title inherited] had already taken my father's eldest brother Sidney into his firm and when, at the age of 19, my father qualified as a mining engineer, Sir John took him into his firm as well.

With an eye on the colonial market, Sir John had seen an opening for the sale of his ploughs and his windmills in South Africa, so when my father was 21 he sent him with his brother Sidney to the Cape Colony to establish the sale of his machinery in South Africa. He tacked my father's name on to his own firm and called it Howard Farrar and Company.

From the Cape my father went to Barberton in the Lowveld to install the first mill for the Union Gold Company.

My father's rigorous upbringing, plus the sound common sense and the frugality he had inherited from his mother, were the qualities most likely to be of help to him as a pioneer in a new and raw country.

Having arrived at the Cape, he went by a small coastal steamer to Port Elizabeth, which in those days was little better than a small underdeveloped settlement. He and his brother expanded the scope of the Howard business over the whole of the Eastern Province, selling his uncle's ploughs, windmills and other machinery.

In those days, to quote from the sketch written by one who knew my father well, he was 'an athlete, a springy, lissom runner, with stamina also a feature'. He held, for 25 years, the South African record for a mile. The river, too, attracted him, for he was a good swimmer and could also handle a pair of oars with efficiency and ease. A first class cross country rider, he won the several point to points in later life.

My father was 19 when he arrived in South Africa and he remained in the Cape Colony for the next seven years. Seven very happy years, I believe, because his expanding business took him to every part of the Cape Colony, where in his leisure time he could shoot and fish to his heart's content and train for his athletics. He continued to run until 1890 when he was defeated in a quarter mile race in Johannesburg.

From East London he went to Barberton. In those days Barberton could only be reached from the coast at Lourenco Marques (ed. note: now Maputo). It was a

10 day trek through fever infested country with native porters. Gold had been discovered in the Barberton district and my father before long controlled certain concessions in order to float his companies. It was beautiful hilly country, with shooting and good fishing, but the Barberton goldmines were not as productive as had been expected and in 1886 he moved on to the Rand. The journey from Barberton to Johannesburg was extremely expensive in those days. The post cart, with a team of six horses, made the journey in 3 to 4 days. The team was changed at the different post stations and one journey accounted for 200 horses or mules to complete the journey.

My father was 27 when he made the journey and arrived on the Rand. The bleak high veldt and the turmoil of a mining camp and the peace of the small mining community at Barberton, must have been a very unpleasant change. It must equally had been a tremendous challenge to a young man of his age, but, at the same time, he had this advantage over many of the get rich quick speculators who thronged to Johannesburg at the time, he was a qualified mining engineer, with already a considerable knowledge of gold mining and its problems from his time in Barberton. Added to this, sound common sense and unbounding energy, a tremendous capacity for hard, concentrated work and tenacity of purpose.

So many men who had gone there to make their fortunes, fell by the wayside or became discouraged and left, many without even enough money to pay their fare to the Cape.

My father pulled out of the mining camp and concentrated his activities on the part of the reef some distance from the main mine where as yet gold had not been confirmed. His conjecture proved to be right and he founded East Rand Proprietary Mines of which, before he married in 1892, he had become Chairman and Managing Director.

CHAPTER 2

My mother always said that it was the only time my father lost his reason when, at the last moment, in March 1896, he was persuaded to throw in his lot with the Reform Committee. He was the last to join. The true history of the Jameson Raid is lost in a maze of plot and counterplot. To what extent the reformers were merely a pawn in the game of chess played by Cecil Rhodes and President Kruger against each other can only be surmised. It was a clash between a pastoral, proud and independent race, against a pulsing, progressive, industrial new population.

These newcomers, or the Uitlanders as they were named by the Boers had been drawn to the Transvaal by its mineral wealth with the promise of fortunes to be made out of the gold embedded within the quartz of the newly discovered reef.

They came from their respective countries, where they had enjoyed a voice in the government of their own countries, and they therefore felt that they were entitled to a say in the government of their adopted country. They argued that through the development of the mineral wealth of the Transvaal, plus the millions of capital entrusted to them by European investors, they had created a new and rich South Africa, far removed from the poor pastoral country it had been before their arrival. The Boers themselves had benefited in more ways than one by this foreign capital. The Uitlanders had purchased farms from them, for a price far in excess of the value of the land and beyond their wildest dreams and yet, although the Uitlanders were pouring money into the pockets of the Republic, they had absolutely no say in the government of the country. The Uitlanders had a just grievance, but President Kruger had no love for the British. As a boy of 12 he had taken part in the Great Trek when the Boers had felt themselves pushed out of the Cape by the English.

They had packed their families and their belongings into the ox wagons, and trekked off into the blue, experiencing untold hardships. Some settled in the Transvaal and formed their independent republic far removed, they believed, from the interference of the detested Uitlanders. No wonder President Kruger was determined to keep his independence at all costs and to hold the Uitlanders at bay come what may. He was wise enough to know that many of them were not here to stay, but merely to make what they could from the country and return whence they came. Interviewed by a reporter in 1887 he was asked if he did not consider that an intelligent man with a stake in the country, whatever his nationality should not be entitled to have a voice in the affairs of the country through representation on the legislative.

"The President was sitting in an armchair and received me wearily", the reporter states, "he settled down to vigorous smoking through a long German pipe, a maid brought us tea. Later the President cleared his nose in a manner peculiar to himself. 'If it is within the law it can be done,' he said, 'if it is not in compliance with the law, it cannot be done. Wealth cannot break the law. A man would have to stay 20 to 40 years in the country to earn that representation.'"

In 1892 he showed signs of a change of thought, when he stated that he desired to add to the burghers of the state, but he would only look for the people who had been obedient to the laws of the country and it would make no difference between rich man and poor men, only between good men and bad men. So, over the years President Kruger had promised and counter promised. Away back in 1882 he had promised that full rights of citizenship would be given after five years of residence in the Republic. But in 1895 the problem was still unsolved and the position was such that no Uitlander could ever hope to attain these rights in full and his children, although born in the Republic, would remain aliens like himself. The next year a petition signed by 32,000 inhabitants was rejected by the Volksraad with scornful laughter and so the agitation and frustration grew, until it reached boiling point in the autumn of 1895, when all it needed was a spark to set the whole Rand ablaze.

The boards themselves were divided on the subject, the middle party headed by General Joubert believed that the Uitlanders were entitled to the franchise and unless it were granted, trouble was bound to follow.

Like the Uitlanders, Cecil Rhodes had come up against a brick wall. President Kruger and the Republic were the supreme obstacle to his dream of South African unity. He wanted to open the way to the north for his railways, so after a stormy interview with Kruger in 1894 on Cape and Transvaal relations, he admitted the hopelessness of ever coming to any form of agreement with the President. It was a clash of personalities. Kruger went too slowly at the pace of his ox wagons, and Rhodes did everything too fast, owing to his bad health he was working against time and he had neither diplomacy, statesmanship or tact. He cut ruthlessly through every obstacle to further his aims. But President Kruger was the nut that he could not crack, and in 1895 it was railway politics which brought his failure to come to an agreement with the President to a head.

Kruger wanted his port in Delagoa Bay (ed. note: now Maputo Bay) and until he could accomplish this, he would not allow any other railway into his country. Left to themselves Boers would not have had a yard of railway lines within their border, they were not interested in railways. But the Uitlanders had created a community which could not be fed by ox wagons. Johannesburg had been threatened by famine in 1894 because of the drought the oxen could not make the journey to the railhead.

The railway from the Cape had been thrust by Rhodes through the Free State to the very borders of the Republic, only 50 miles from the mines, and all the supplies and machinery for the mines had to come by ox wagon from the border.

Then Kruger closed the two drifts over which the ox wagons had to bring the goods dumped on the border by the railway. Truckloads of goods piled up on the border and Johannesburg was in despair.

Towards the autumn of 1895 the tension in Johannesburg was so explosive that Kruger could not ignore the possibility of an open revolt and he tentatively agreed to negotiate terms with the Uitlanders. The plot was hatched.

The Uitlanders were determined to make a demand for the franchise once and for all, and this time if they were refused, they in their turn would refuse to recognise the government officials and they would appeal to the Boers as a whole, many of whom were in favour of compromise.

This plot was to hold the town Johannesburg, which, after all, they had built, owned and occupied. To this end they imported food and arms, the Reform Committee came into being. That they wanted to hold a pistol at Kruger's head is clear and that they did not intend insurrection against the Republic, in the beginning, is certain. It was originally a gigantic game of bluff which they believed they could get away with. The sole aim was the redress of their grievances.

They had not planned to seize Johannesburg with the Union Jack flying but to frighten Kruger into submission of their rights. But, as time went on, the plot thickened. They decided to issue an ultimatum to Kruger. On its being treated with the usual contempt, they would take possession of Johannesburg and the same night seize the state arsenal and the seat of government at Pretoria and appeal to the whole of South Africa to see that their wrongs were righted.

They thought they could do this without a shot being fired, if it could be done by complete surprise, so the success of the enterprise depended on absolute secrecy. Help from outside they must have, so they appealed to Cecil Rhodes. At this point the plot became reality, Cecil Rhodes swept into the arena and the Reform Committee became the pawns in a game of higher politics centred round Cecil Rhodes, with the probable connivance of Chamberlain.

In all the books that have been written about Jameson Raid, very little has ever been said to explain the reluctance of the reform leaders; my father, Lionel Phillips, John Hays Hammond and Percy Fitzpatrick and Frank Rhodes (Cecil's brother) to bring about the open insurrection in Johannesburg which they were expected to accomplish by Cecil Rhodes and Dr Jim [Jameson].

Cecil Rhodes must have thought that there was every chance that the leaders could bring off their coup with his help from outside and he overestimated their capacity in the role of full scale revolutionaries. They were men who had made fortunes in the last 10 years, they were all respected in the mining industry. They were exasperated and frustrated by cruelties refusing to give them the franchise but I doubt that their grievances were so great as to launch them into full-scale revolution. Cecil Rhodes, on the other hand, was a visionary with an unfulfilled idea and was prepared to ride roughshod over any obstacle that stood between him and his goal of a united South Africa. If Dr Jameson had been the leader of the Reform committee in Johannesburg and Cecil Rhodes the invading force, they would more than likely have succeeded where the more cautious leaders failed.

Once Cecil Rhodes entered into the plot, all the people involved were swept forward to its disastrous conclusion.

I believe that my father was persuaded to join at the last minute, being the largest employer of labour on the Rand, in direct touch with importing machinery in bulk to the mines, who was the obvious cover for smuggling arms into the republic.

With his help, the trouble of getting arms through was removed. Rifles were smuggled in under the excuse that the De Beers company, of which Cecil was chairman, was supplying the gold mines with coke. Three sheep wagons got through loaded with 800 rifles, covered with a load of coke, only four days before Jameson crossed the border, and others were smuggled in oil drums. My mother always told us that my father worked all night in his shirt sleeves unloading trucks. Rifles were still being unloaded as Dr Jim rode towards Johannesburg. Kruger was an old man in 1896, the Abraham of his people, dogged, obstinate and obdurate.

Cecil Rhodes was a comparatively young man, the son of a clergyman and a giant in the new progressive, industrial world. A fanatical imperialist, as fanatical in his way as Kruger was in his. There was absolutely no meeting point between them and it was a fight distinguish between opposing ideals and loyalties.

Each to each other was the rock on which they both foundered, all the rest were merely pawns in a game. If they could have got together who knows how much misery could have been averted and who knows what the peaceful development of South Africa might have been. Kruger died alone in exile in Switzerland in 1903 and Cecil Rhodes died in his cottage in Muizenberg in 1902 and the breach between the English and the Dutch races in South Africa would continue to fester.

Kruger was the ogre who dominated our lives in South Africa when we were children. We were fascinated by the stories about him, so we visualised him with his square top hat and his pipe and his straggly unkempt beard. He was the enemy who had imprisoned my father and who was responsible for the Boer War and for my father having to leave us to go and fight. We regarded Cecil Rhodes with awe, not unmixed with a sense of resentment that in some way, which we did not understand, he had done some injury to my father, which was too large and undefined for our understanding. Once, when we were very small, my mother took us to tea with Cecil Rhodes. We were on our best behaviour and perched stiffly on chairs on the stoep. He sat in a comfortable chair in a grey creased suit. I have the impression that he was a big untidy man. We were tongue tied and ill at ease. He did not speak to us and we were pleased when it was time to leave. Even my mother was not her usual bright, gay self. But I remember more vividly then than anything else the hydrangeas spreading like a blue carpet beneath the oak trees, the sun light and dark shadows cast across the grass and the slopes of Table Mountain in the background, and the cool of the pillared stoep and the shadowed depth of the panelled book-lined room behind us and the silent, not unfriendly, awe inspiring, untidy, large man, relaxed yet so dominant that we found we were overpowered and speechless. I believe that at the time of the Jameson Raid my mother went to see Cecil Rhodes to try and persuade him to not to take any action against the Republic and she undoubtedly did everything she could to dissuade my father from joining the Reform Committee, without any success. Dr Jameson, like Cecil, had gone to South Africa for his health. At the time of the raid, he was administrator of Matabeleland on the borders of the Transvaal. His career in South Africa had been one of unbroken success. He had acted with courage and leadership in the Matabele war. He was impulsive and reckless and drew men like a magnet by his charm and personality. Once Cecil Rhodes stepped into the arena it became a battle of the giants. Kruger was the giant of a pastoral people; the Bible was his textbook and the Boers were the tribes of Israel with their flocks of sheep he had led through the desert to the promised land.

The founder of his family had arrived at the Cape with the Dutch East India Company in 1713. In 1835, when he was 10 years old, he was with his parents on the Great Trek. He fought and hunted with the men and learned to read and write from the Old Testament of the family Bible which was the only literature he knew and, like many of the old Boer leaders he learnt to believe in divine guidance and to put his trust in God. When he was 25 he went off by himself into the veldt for several days. He himself stated that, during those days in the wilderness, God had communed with him and conferred on him his special favour. Throughout his life he professed his faith in God's guidance. He persuaded himself that any cause he chose to take was the one directed by God.

At the age of 14 he had already fought against the Matabele and the Zulus and at the age of 17 he was a field cornet and in 1880 he was elected president of the Transvaal.

The American's wife [to whom Muriel is referring must remain a mystery], in her memoirs, says that she went to see Kruger during the Jameson Raid.

'At last he stood up on his feet, tall and upright, his head thrown back and in a voice like thunder said, in Dutch,

'Speak, Lord, thy servant heareth' then he sat down. A while later he said,

'God has not yet spoken. I tell my generals to show mercy on the battlefields, but the penalty of murder is death. If a man sets a dog on another man, one does not kick the dog but the man. I do not want the Reform Committee. I want Cecil Rhodes. If England would give me Cecil Rhodes they could have the Transvaal.'

The stage was set, the plot was hatched. Dr Jim moved to the border of the Transvaal with an armed force waiting to rush to the assistance of the Reform committee in Johannesburg should the situation arise when the lives of the women and children were in jeopardy. But on no account was he to invade the Transvaal unless he received word from the Reform committee.

Dr Jim was not the man to play a waiting game. He was Sir Galahad and all the Knights of the Round Table rolled into one. His was the role of rushing in where angels fear to tread, of desperate hazards, of success against fearful odds, of shock tactics. He could not visualise defeat.

Meanwhile the Reform Committee in Johannesburg hesitated. The date for the coup had been fixed for December 28, 1896. The success of their venture depended on absolute secrecy. My father said that they learned that Kruger became fully aware of the plot and was playing a waiting game. Further, they had forgotten that the date fixed for their coup at Nacht had stalled. And Pretoria was overflowing with Boer farmers who had come into Pretoria from all over the Transvaal,

Camping with their families and all armed with the rifle which was as a part of them as a walking stick is to a farmer.

So they sent hectic messages to Dr Jim, "Do not come", they said "at any cost". At the last minute they had also realised that they had not nearly enough arms and ammunition for their purpose and as far as they were concerned the plot had virtually fizzled out.

But the initiative was no longer in their hands. Dr Jameson was not the man to be deflected from his course once he had taken the bit between his teeth. He had with him a force of over 200 Mashonaland mounted police, all highly trained men and a number of foot soldiers.

In the past he had succeeded and other revolutions had had less justification than this one. If he, Dr Jim, could bring this off he would not only be a local hero but would have the sympathy of many people outside the Republic and there was his friend Cecil Rhodes whose imperial aims had been so thwarted by the Republic and who had set so much store on the success of this venture. What would he feel if Dr Jim failed him at the last minute? Once the leaders in Johannesburg realised he was on his way they would be bound to carry out their part of the agreement and there was nothing to prevent a coup and he must have agreed.

So Dr Jim harangued his troops. He told them that they were marching on Johannesburg to protect the women and children and as an insurrection in Johannesburg was imminent, and he proceeded to cut all the telegraph lines.

On a hot afternoon on December 30, 1896 when the leading conspirators were gathered together in Johannesburg, they received a telegram which made their blood run cold. It read, "The contractor has started on the earthworks with 700 men" but the wires had been cut and his telegram arrived too late.

The Reform Committee sprang into action. They handed out what arms they had to the miners and took measures to keep order. Trainloads of refugees, fleeing from possible trouble, left the station packed to the roof. Earthworks were thrown up and there were feverish preparations made to defend the town.

My mother was sent to the Cape, as were the other wives of the other leaders. She would not leave my father, although she often told us that through these hectic days and nights, she never saw a sight of him and

Christmas Day came and went unnoticed, while in the heat of midsummer she sat at home, day after day, and worried and waited for every scrap of news.

The High Commissioner, hearing the news that Jameson was marching on Johannesburg repudiated his action and sent a messenger to order him back, but nothing could stop Dr Jim once he had started and he took no notice of the order. On the fourth day he was trapped. The Boers knew just how to handle such a situation. They assembled their commandos with great speed and positioned them between Jameson and his goal. Further resistance was useless. The invaders were outnumbered and outmanoeuvered. Dr Jim sent frantic messages to the reform leaders to send him help, but no help was forthcoming and there was nothing left to do but surrender. The same night the invaders were all lodged in Pretoria jail.

In Johannesburg, when news that Dr Jim was on his way was made public, excitement spread like wildfire through the waiting crowds. Women gathered flowers to throw before the conquering heroes, men rushed to join the reformers, many of whom were armed only with walking sticks. When the bitter truth was out at last and Jameson had surrendered, frenzy seized the waiting crowds. 'Why had the forces been kept in town?' they wanted to know: Why has no relief been sent out to Jameson? Jameson became the hero of the day and the leaders of the reform committee took the brunt of the fury of the crowds.

The fate of the reformers in the Transvaal was sealed. Her Majesty's Commissioner had wired to the Boer government, the people of Johannesburg would lay down their arms and if they did not comply, they would forfeit all claim to sympathy from her Majesty's government and from British subjects all over the world as the lives of Jameson and the prisoners are now practically in their hands.

The Boer government had agreed to hand Dr Jim and all his men over to the High Commissioner provided Johannesburg immediately disarmed. And so ended the Jameson Raid.

De Keiwist says of the raid that it was inexcusable and its folly and unforgivable in its consequences. A British force operating from British territory invaded a country with which the Queen was at peace. It did not do so in sufficient strength to have any chance of success. The raid was supposed to assist a revolution organised in Johannesburg yet the revolutionaries had given Jameson the most emphatic orders not to move. The blame must fall mostly on Rhodes. He encouraged and financed the movement yet failed to control the people he supported. Jameson, having taken part in other of Rhodes' irregular military ventures in Rhodesia, naturally supposed that he would have Rhodes' support over his decision to invade the Transvaal. Had he ever received the telegram which Rhodes sent he might have altered his decision.

Rhodes was at a lunch party at Groote Schuure when the news had reached him of Jameson's surrender. Pacing up and down his library he kept repeating, "Poor old Jim has upset my applecart."

The failure of the Reform Committee to back up Jameson's disastrous raid is simple. It was a question of the Union Jack. Quoting from Elizabeth Parkinson's book on the Jameson Raid she says,

Charles Leonard arrived at the Groote Schuure on Saturday December 28 determined to put things right at worst. The Johannesburgers would not have the English flag on Christmas Day. He said George Farrar had come round to his house at 7 o'clock in the morning and said, "I hear if Jameson comes he is going to hoist the Union Jack. I have induced every man who has joined me and who is helping me in the business to go in on the basis that we want a reformed Republic. Farrar then went on to take a solemn pledge every word of which Leonard remembered. "This" he said "is Boer country. It would be absolutely wrong to do anything else and I will not go a yard further in the business unless this basis is maintained."

It is my belief that my father never deviated from his resolution that a reformed Republic was the sole and only aim of the rising.

There is no doubt that taking advantage of Kruger's dislike of the British, Germany was angling with Kruger with the aim of getting a stake in the Republic.

Rhodes, with the connivance of Chamberlain, and foreseeing the danger of such alliance, was given the perfect excuse of annexing the Transvaal by a lightning coup, under the British flag, by secretly financing and backing the plans for a rising in Johannesburg by the Uitlanders.

It is possible that Lionel Phillips, Percy Fitzpatrick and Frank Rhodes who after all was Rhodes' brother would have agreed to this change of front and allow themselves to be overridden by Rhodes, for without the help of Dr Jameson's Armed Forces of mounted Bechuanaland police on the borders, camped on land under the administration of the charter company would have been impossible. Although his plan was not in the original concept of the Uitlanders instigators, It was probably forced on them by Cecil Rhodes.

But my father was absolutely adamant that the rising was aimed entirely to overthrow Kruger with the object of a change of government with moderate Boers to redress the grievances of the Uitlanders and was on no condition to be aimed at this seizure of the Transvaal under the British flag which could only end in the full scale civil war. The disruption of the whole country would not be in the interests of the Uitlanders and the Reform Committee in Johannesburg was completely unprepared and unarmed for such an eventuality.

My father never underestimated the courage or the tenacity of the Boers, who under such circumstances would stand solidly behind Kruger, extremists and moderates alike, to protect the Transvaal Republic from an act of aggression none of them would countenance. It is quite clear by the statement made by my father to Charles Leonard and quoted that these were my father's views. There is no question in my mind that the reason why the Reform Committee at the last moment sent messages to Dr Jim to postpone his invasion and not to cross the border at any cost was not based on timidity but entirely on the policy on which last-minute disagreement with Rhodes' policy.

Dr Jameson was handed over to the British government and returned to England where he was tried and sentenced to 18 months in prison, but owing to his health he only served four months and Rhodes return to England to answer an enquiry.

Sixty-four members of the Reform Committee and four leaders; my father, Frank Rhodes, John Hays Hammond and Lionel Phillips were taken to Pretoria to jail to be tried under Roman Dutch law, on a charge of high treason.

It must have been after the South African War that Dr Jim came to stay at Chicheley. We met so many people when we were children and we always held a sort of enquiry upon them amongst ourselves. Our likes and dislikes were not entirely instinctive for we had a sort of yardstick; shoes were one of the most important. In the days when most men had their shoes made-to-measure we could tell at a glance between the London shoemakers, Peel, Lobb and Metcalf. It did not matter how old the shoes were, but uncared-for shoes ruled the wearer out as far as we were concerned. We were not conscious of Dr Jim's shoes because he absolutely fascinated us. His eyes were large and very wide apart and he had a very high forehead. When he came down after tea we went straight to look for him. We would find him slumped in an armchair smoking endless cigarettes. He never seemed to have any matches and was always hunting in his pockets. My mother kept matchboxes in all the spare bedrooms and to make sure they stayed there, each matchbox was slipped into an enamel cover with 'Bedroom' written in large letters on the lid. One evening when we were downstairs, Dr Jim was pursuing his usual hunt for his matches. When at last out of his pocket came the box with 'Bedroom' on the lid. My mother swooped on the box. "Now I know where all the matchboxes out of the bedroom go to!" she laughed. Dr Jim gave us a conspiratorial smile. Although we had played no part in the conspiracy, we immediately felt drawn onto his side and we would willingly have gone and fetched any other illegal box from any of the bedrooms to help him, but we conspired with each other to keep him supplied, not an easy task in a large house when boxes of matches were left lying about. But there were a number of empty enamel holders in the bedrooms after our raids.

He never even asked us and I do not remember that he took any notice of us but he captured our interest more than many of the people we met. This was Dr Jim as I knew him 10 years after the Jameson Raid, in failing health, but still with the ability to draw all and sundry to him.

CHAPTER 3

For four of the hottest months of the year from January 9 to June 15, 1896 my father and the reformers were in Pretoria jail.

The jail was intended for native prisoners and had up till then not been used for white prisoners. It was an open space about 400 ft.² enclosed by a high wall, with small badly ventilated sleeping cells built along the wall. Sanitation and water were practically nil and the cells were crawling with vermin. The prisoners slept on the floor and washed in the yard from a trickle of water that ran down an open gutter. The urinals were three closets and six buckets between the 250 prisoners, black and white, which sometimes were only emptied once in four days. The sun beat down on the crowded open yard, when the temperature was up to 103 in the shade, but there was no shade for the prisoners from the glaring heat. The prison governor, a man called Du Plessis was a relation of Kruger's with an unkempt beard and bloodshot eyes and on the face of it he did nothing to alleviate the plight of the reformers.

'The reform leaders' said Bauer quoting from E. Parkinson's book on the Jameson Raid, 'represented 40 million sterling, moreover they were hospitable, cultivated, the most popular men in Johannesburg. It was a sign of Kruger's untutored ignorance that he treated such expensive materials so roughly.'

I remember my father saying that Du Plessis was not above taking bribes and therefore he and the other three, Lionel Phillips, Frank Rhodes and Hays Hammond, were able to have food smuggled into them. Otherwise the prison fare consisted mainly of mealy meal out of a wooden bowl. Although it probably cost a lot of money, they managed to get along reasonably well. In her book of reminiscences, Chapin says, 'We managed to smuggle food into the prisoners. I remember one American woman concealing sausages in her leg-of-mutton sleeve which was the fashion at that time.' Personally I think the smuggling must have been none under the benevolence and bloodshot eyes of Du Plessis.

Quoting from the newspaper, "For the first two days these gentlemen were kept without water and their food consisted of mealy pap served without spoons. It was very funny to hear how these men reared in comfort, most probably in luxury, reluctantly dipped their untrained fingers into the hot mess. It was a slow process, after which they were regaled with stewed goat in a pannikin full of nasty gravy in which it was boiled. This twice a day, in a climate with the temperature of one hundred and three in the shade, no wonder that Du Plessis reaped a harvest. Even in 1880 the prison was so invaded by hungry insects that a fever, which broke out there at the time and which closely resembled typhoid, was pronounced bug fever as having been caused by the poisonous bites of the voracious vermin. Why does not the government not set fire to the precious building and erect a new prison?"

"I went to the prison", the report continues, "and showed my pass. 'You can have five minutes'. I was escorted by a very genial young Dutch giant who took me to the forlorn, broken-down cottage. In a tiny room without any furniture, but a small deal table and a chair or two were Col Rhodes, George Farrar and Mr. Phillips. They were in their shirtsleeves. They were pleased to see me. In five minutes the Boer giant came to tell me my time was up. George Farrar seized half a loaf of bread and with an unerring aim threw it at the giants. I thought it was a splendid joke and exploded in laughter. He went away and I was left with my friends for another quarter of an hour. Colonel Rhodes went out of the room and returned with a huge bouquet of flowers in one hand and a basket of figs which had been sent in by friends, with which he was highly delighted. The four leaders were kept strictly apart from the other 64 members of the reformers. My father and Frank Rhodes were the only two out of the four leaders who were never ill during their imprisonment. The Boers, for all the bad conditions in the jail, were far from being indifferent to the health of their prisoners.

John Hays Hammond, who became very ill, was removed and kept under guard in a house where his wife could look after him, and Lionel Phillips, suffering from a cold was given the same treatment, but he insisted on returning, which leaves the impression that, had he insisted on health reasons, he too could have enjoyed better living conditions.

No doubt that the reformers made a lot of propaganda out of the terrible conditions in the jail and in consequence public opinion all over South Africa and in England veered in sympathy with their plight and those Uitlanders who had kept aloof and had taken no active part in the rising, rose in wrath and sent petitions to Kruger to plead for leniency on their behalf. Kruger had all the cards in his hand, with one hand on his Bible, he played a game of cat and mouse with all of them, inflicting on the reformers a long drawn out mental torture, by giving them no inkling of what their ultimate fate would be. Barney Barnato was one of the first to take up the cudgels. Almost the most colourful figure in the early days of the diamond mines, where he had arrived from the east end of London, his only possession in the world being one large box of cigars, from the proceeds of which he amassed a fortune. He went to see Kruger, dressed in black from head to foot, he threatened to close all the mines controlled by the Barnato brothers, and further to sell out all his interests in the Transvaal if Kruger would not deal leniently with the reformers.

Not many years afterwards on a voyage back to England with his two nephews Solly and Wolf Joel, poor Barney fell overboard and was drowned. My father told us this story when we were children. We never met Solly and Joel, but we had seen pictures of him always with a mauve orchid in his buttonhole. We wondered if he felt as sorry as we did for this little man with the great heart and a box of cigars. At the time Solly may not have been so pleased with his uncle, the way in which his uncle rushed in to defend the reformers, but there is no doubt that Kruger listened to him. For if Barney had carried out his threat, the gold production of the Rand would have been reduced, thus indirectly reducing by a very substantial sum the revenue of the state.

My mother, Mrs. Lionel Phillips and Mrs. Hays Hammond and the wives of the other reformers did what they could to augment the prison rations, by taking food to their husbands, or, like the lady with the muttonchop sleeves, smuggling sweets and even half a bottle of whiskey hidden within their voluminous clothing.

But my mother could not make the uncomfortable journey from Johannesburg to Pretoria very often because she was pregnant. I often wonder what my mother's feelings must have been because she never spoke about those nerve wracking days. She was 25 at the time, attractive, full of courage and good to look at. She had met my father on the boat going out to South Africa in 1891. Her brother-in-law, Bell who became the Head of Bell's asbestos and her sister, had taken her with them on their business voyage. This was my mother's great adventure. The ships in those days were very small and very uncomfortable by our standards, but they took very little longer to make the journey to the Cape than they do today. There was no refrigeration, hence no fresh food, or fresh milk, unless the passengers could afford to take their own cow on board and the heat in the cabins through the tropics was stifling. In rough weather the little ships rolled and pitched and wallowed through the Atlantic seas.

On the way out, seasickness took a heavy toll of the less experienced travellers, until the dreaded Bay of Biscay had been crossed and the welcome port of Madeira reached. From then on most of the passengers had gained their sea legs and the rest of the voyage was given up to deck games and evening dances. At Madeira the cabin trunks came out of the hold with a load of summer clothes under the winter clothes were put away. The little ship, without any communication from the outside world, became a self-contained unit. Lifelong friendships were made and broken as she docked and the passengers went on their way. But my mother's shipboard romance with my father lasted for 25 years. They were married in Johannesburg in 1892.

My father, already established at the age of 32, was one of the most influential mining magnates on the Rand. My mother, brought up in Ireland on milk and potatoes, had a great deal in common. Neither had ever had any money when they were young, they both had tremendous energy and vitality and great courage and above all they both had wonderful health. I never knew either of them to be ill. My father was one of the fittest men I ever knew and he took a tremendous amount of exercise, either riding, playing tennis, golf or any form of violent exercise, like cutting down trees or wielding an axe. He taught us to ride, to swim, to run and to jump. It was part of his weekend's enjoyment to train us to be athletes.

It must have been wonderful for my mother when she married my father to be able to spend money, but in Johannesburg there was nothing to buy and no amount of money could establish a gracious way of living in a mining town. Their first home was a tin bungalow on

Hospital Hill. My mother used to tell us that it was the first reasonable house to be built in Johannesburg. Hospital Hill was so named because the first tin hospital dominated the cluster of a rocky prominence jutting up above the endless plains of the high veldt.

Except for the well built office blocks, Johannesburg was in those days a platter of tin shanties. The streets were mud tracks in the summer and knee deep in red dust in the winter and the high wheeled uncomfortable Cape carts drawn by two horses the only means of transport.

Water was very scarce and living conditions primitive to the extreme. Eggs were six shillings a dozen and green vegetables almost impossible to obtain at any price and a cabbage was considered a great luxury. Flowers were impossible to buy in the winter. At night the tin shanties and the bars overflowed with a teeming crowd of men of all nationalities, typical of any mining camp in any other part of the world.

For six months during the winter not a drop of rain fell on the parched soil and everything was dried up and baked brown. The red dust penetrated everything, every inch and cranny in the houses and the dust storms when the wind blew were as dense as a London fog. Then the thunderclouds gathered. Down came the rain, turning the dusty tracks into a sea of red sticky mud and the gullies that had been as dry as a bone all the winter became raging torrents.

Almost overnight the veldt became a vivid green and the wild flowers sprang up everywhere, and with the rains came the insects and mosquitoes and the snakes from their winter holes on the rocks.

The most modern bungalows were cased in by wire gauze netting to prevent the snakes and insects getting into the houses, but the sound of the torrential rain on the tin roof was deafening and it was impossible to sleep at night for the noise. There is no twilight in South Africa, the sun sets at 6 o'clock and rises at 6 o'clock all year round and the minute the sun sets it is dark. Even today South Africans start the day much earlier than we do in England and go to bed correspondingly earlier than in European countries because there is no twilight and the evenings are very long.

Sometime before my eldest sister Helen was born, my father took my mother back to England and my sister was born in London in October 1894. They stayed at the Hyde Park Hotel and my mother had a wonderful spending spree. She could now buy her clothes from all the most expensive shops and stay in all the most comfortable hotels. She was gay and full of life and must have enjoyed every moment. She would have loved her own house in London. Why not? Some of the other South African millionaires had already bought houses in Park Lane or in the country and had no intention of living in South Africa. Before they were married my father visited England entirely on business and after going to see his mother in Bedford he had returned to Johannesburg to his work and all his interests were centred on the development of his various projects in South Africa.

I am sure he had no intention of making his home anywhere else, so back they went to Johannesburg, my mother took with her an English nanny to look after my sister Helen, and trunks full of the most expensive clothes, furniture, china and glass and they moved from Hospital Hill to a better house in Doornfontein, on the outskirts of the town, where my mother, with undaunted gaiety, proceeded to make the best time she could. But the tension in Johannesburg was growing. My father became more and more involved with the grievances of the Uitlanders and there must have been days when my mother hardly saw him.

Then came the day in January 1896 when he was arrested and sent to Pretoria in jail. My mother was unable to make the tedious uncomfortable journey to Pretoria to see him, she needed all her courage to endure those weary days. Not a very auspicious time to have been born, I really could not have chosen a worse moment, with my mother worried to death and my father in prison. It had only this advantage, that when I grew older I was able to cause consternation amongst other children by telling them that I was born when my father was in prison.

My mother told me that my father was allowed out of prison under the escort of the Boer giants to come and see me and he spent the whole day tidying up the backyard. Frank Rhodes was my one and only godparent. Ten years later I remember him coming to stay at Chicheley. He was a great favourite of us children. He had grey hair and a grey moustache and a twinkle in his eyes. His face was a network of deep lines and he used to entertain us by making faces. He could contort his face like pressing a rubber ball into the most extraordinary expressions. He was a great friend of my father and it was always a red letter day when he came to stay.

History does not relate that he too was allowed out of prison to come and see his godchild, but Du Plessis, the governor of the prison must have been far more humane than one has been led to suppose and I am sure that the giant Boer escort was regaled by plenty of food and drink as they watched my father tidy the backyard.

CHAPTER 4

As soon as my father had been arrested, his brother Percy had returned to South Africa to do what he could to help, and during the five months he was there, he wrote weekly reports to my grandmother. On the February 8th he wrote, 'I went over to see George, but only through a board window, as the regulated number of visitors for the week had been exhausted several times. The guards are very decent fellows. The Dutch are well disposed and civil, in fact one can hardly imagine that there has been any trouble at all'.

In February, he wrote, 'They are now in a very comfortable house in the best position in the town, of course under guard, but they have their own horses and servants and ride out in the afternoon with the police lieutenant in plain clothes. The officials have been very civil to me and I really hope everything may end in a fine way. There are several hare brained madmen amongst the reformers and in March the reformers were still in their house in the best part of the town.' On May 25 he wrote, 'Probably the sentence will be reduced to 5 years and how much of this they have to serve depends upon whether the English courts punish Jameson. If he escapes, our men will pay for it.'

'I drove out to Doornkop, Jameson's officers must have been utterly incapable, as they had miles and miles of open country, but preferred walking into a broken defile, where the Boers were in ambush. The pursuing Boers at once closed in on their flank and rear and had them at their mercy. '

On May 30, Percy cabled: 'I think we ought to have our reward in a day or two, when I am able to cable you, "All Free!" It will be a very happy day for me. We have had all Africa at work; the last few days petitions tumbling in. I fear we badgered the poor President to death and he will be glad to see the end of the reformers.'

'Reform is dead anyway during the President's lifetime, after such an act, he must be allowed to do just what he likes. My work will be over and I will not be sorry to forget, in the glories of the mountains, all the anxieties of the last five months.'

'Sidney stays here, as George will go home. He needs a change; George has come out of it well. Both sides speak of his pluck and fortitude.'

'On February 7th we returned from the Cape on the Thursday night express having seen Rhodes and Beit, but all they care for is themselves and all the other people in Johannesburg might go to hell.

We went to see the prisoners. They were sitting in shirts and trousers on small wooden boxes round a trunk for a table having a game of whist. The prison is filthy and they sleep on the floor on mattresses without sheets over them. They have a yard about twelve feet square, where they exercise and eat all their meals. They say they are very well treated and have everything they like to eat and drink and books to read, but they have to go to bed at 6 o'clock and have suffered from most fearful heats and have caught 800 bugs and are eaten up all the time. George has had fever but is alright again.

I went to see the Jameson lot who were very down on the Johannesburg lot for not having sent help to them, which to us does seem wrong also. But if they had and Jameson's men had got in, I believe the Boers would have blown up the town.'

'However there is no doubt that there was a terrible amount of bad management somewhere amongst the leaders and the rights and wrongs may come out in the trial. The Boers all through have behaved awfully well and are very brave and plucky men and much too strong for us.'

'Why they were flocking up in their thousands! The most exciting sight! We saw them from the train coming up all the way from the Cape. However, men who have been living out here for years and know all the habits of the Boers and their struggle could have arranged things so stupidly seems impossible to credit.'

I was three weeks old, on 27 April, when my father, Frank Rhodes, Lionel Phillips and John Hayes Hammond were condemned to death.

In the blasting heat of midsummer's day the Market Hall in Pretoria converted for the occasion into a courtroom was packed till there was not even standing room and the heat was stifling. A large number of ladies and prominent people entered by the judge's private entrance, so the news reported.

The judge, Gregorowski, had been brought from the Free State and was reputed to be the harshest judge in the whole of South Africa. The accused sat on the right of the judge and at the close of his summing up and in painful silence before leaders of the Reform Committee were conducted to the dock, which had been draped in black for the occasion. Furthermore, the prison warders were dressed in black like undertakers. In the following order Lionel Phillips, Frank Rhodes, my father and John Hays Hammond were asked by the judge if they had anything to say, why sentence of death should not be passed upon them. The reply in each case was no.

The death sentence was then passed by the judge on the four prisoners. Each in turn bowed as the solemn words were spoken, 'And may God have mercy on your soul.'

The charge was that as citizens of the Republic, they had treated and conspired with Dr Jameson, an alien living outside the boundary of the Republic, to come into the territory at the head of an armed force and make a hostile invasion of the Republic and had armed forces ready to assist him by providing provisions and forage for his horses. To this charge the four leaders pleaded guilty.

Afterwards the judge passed judgment on the 59 members of the Reform Committee. They were to serve two years in the prison at Pretoria with a fine of £2,000 and three years banishment from South Africa.

In defending the accused, Mr. Wessels said, they did nothing to endanger the independence of the country. Petition after petition was rejected and it was made an impossibility to become a burger of the state. A demonstration was made, men were armed, it was an unfortunate step to call Jameson in, but they took some measure to ensure their safety. There is no proof that either Rhodes or Jameson intended to bring the safety of the Republic into danger.

Lionel Phillips, Frank Rhodes and Hammond are important men. Farrar is known throughout South Africa for his work in the mining industry. How could they overthrow the Republic with 480 men they had called over the border?

Mrs. Phillips fainted when the sentence was passed and many of the ladies present had to be removed from the court in a collapsed condition. Then there was a stampede to get out of the building to escape from the oppressive air in the court.

Only the judge smiled. It has been reported that he was particularly anxious to give those reformers what for.

The prisoners were taken back to the prison and the people of South Africa gasped. 'Good God!' Cecil Rhodes exclaimed when he heard the news. 'Kruger would never go to do anything like that.'

And my mother with her two small children, what were her reactions on that night in April when she heard the news? And my father, with the words of the death sentence ringing in his ears, 'To be hanged by the neck until you are dead.'

Even if this were only a part of Kruger's war of nerves against the reformers, what must have been the reaction of those four men when the smiling judge on that stifling afternoon passed sentence of death on them?

My mother and father never spoke about it. I believe for my father it was an end and beginning.

It was the end of the young impetuous man who had seen no further than his own interests. Months in prison gave him time to think. That would have been typical of my father's character. He has made a mistake and he would start to build again.

The effect of the trial on my mother had the exactly opposite effect and caused a rift between her and my father which lasted for 20 years, although it had no effect on their devotion for each other. My mother never settled in South Africa again. After six months or a year she was off again back to England. Sometimes my father went with her, but when he went, he looked upon it as a holiday, but my mother always said she was going 'home' to England. My father, on the other hand, was going 'home' when embarked to South Africa.

And so, for the rest of my father's life they played a game of battledore and shuttlecock and we children travelled endlessly backwards and forwards across the Atlantic, till we knew nearly every ship and every Captain on the Union Castle line. Looking back, I find it impossible to tell, up to the time I was 14, when we were in England and how long we spent in Africa and which of the two was really our home.

I suppose my father knew that it was no good trying to anchor my mother down in South Africa. She was not the sort of person anyone could anchor. A great deal of her charm was her gaiety and her sense of enjoyment and, like most beautiful women, she was hopelessly spoiled by my father. If it made my mother happy to go to England, to England she would go and to please her he spent more time in England than he would ever done otherwise. But there were months when he was alone at the farm near Johannesburg. There is no doubt that my mother taught my father that life should not be just all hard work, and the old adage, 'All work and no play make Jack a dull boy' has a great deal of truth. Everyone, she argued, is entitled to some form of leisure. It was not as if my father could not afford to have a holiday. So, although she did succeed in tearing him away from his beloved South Africa, it was never for very long. Then back he would go to his work and his politics, which after all was his life. Then my mother would return and the house came to life again. There was music and laughter and people, but with all her gaiety, my mother had a hard-core of sound commonsense and a very shrewd judgment of character and my father had a great respect for her opinion, especially of people. Without her help he might never have reached the prominence in the political world that he did, because he was completely lacking in every sense of personal ambition. He was not interested in people unless they had something interesting to contribute, otherwise he could be completely oblivious of their existence and he never remembered their names, or who they were if he met them again.

In politics so much time has to be spent in personal contacts and then meeting people and dedicated men like my father will not waste what, in their opinion, is valuable time, in this way. This is where my mother, with her love of entertaining and her interest in people was able to help him. She was the perfect foil to my father's seriousness and a wonderful hostess.

On the last agonising day of the trial, the people of Johannesburg were in a torment. It was decided that the following day should be kept as a day of mourning. The Stock exchange closed and many of the business houses, shops and places of entertainment. Barney, who was the director of De Beers diamond mines in Kimberley wired that the mines should stop working for the day.

Barney, in his black clothes, went to see Kruger and told him that he could not possibly carry on his gold mines in Johannesburg because most of his key men were amongst the reformers who had been sentenced to 2 years imprisonment. So how could he, Barney, carry on without them? Including the fact that John Hayes Hammond was the most distinguished mining engineer on the Rand and he, Barney, was responsible for bringing him to South Africa from America. Also his young nephew, Solly, was amongst the prisoners. In fact, how could the whole economy of the gold mining industry carry on at all if the leading mining magnates were to be executed?

Barney threatened, pleaded, who will ever really know to what extent this little Jew from the east end of London influenced Kruger in his decision? The Bible says 'an eye for and eye and a tooth for a tooth', but it also says 'if your enemy smite you, turn the other cheek.' Whichever part of the Old Testament Kruger quoted to serve his purpose, the following day, after 24 hours of terrifying suspense, Kruger used his authority as President of the Republic to commute the death sentence on the four leaders to 15 years imprisonment.

The first agony was over, but Kruger continued to play his game of cat and mouse with the reform leaders. Meanwhile, in the prison, Du Plessis was insisting on better conditions for his reluctant prisoners. Never had his prison received so many distinguished visitors.

Throughout May, Barney continued to see Kruger. At one interview with him in the beginning of June he said that he felt like a child advising his father, but he reminded his Honour that these men were his friends and if clemency were done, then it were better done quickly.

The President, who, as usual had his hands on his Bible, said, "This is my book, allow me to carry out my work as it and my heart dictates and all will come right."

Barney later on said that he had the greatest admiration for the President. He was a grand old statesman, with a heart as large as his brain. There and then he wrote out a cheque for £50,000 as his contribution towards any fines that the President thought fit to impose on the prisoners. President Kruger did think fit to impose fines on the prisoners to augment his exchequer.

At the beginning of June after nearly five months of imprisonment he issued his verdict. God had spoken at last. The four leaders would be immediately released on the payment of the enormous sum of £25,000 each with a choice of 15 years ban on politics or banishment.

And the other reformers were also offered immediate release on the payment of fines and three years ban on politics.

Cecil Rhodes is reputed to have paid the fines of the 54 members of the reformers.

The four leaders paid, but Frank Rhodes preferred banishment to a ban on politics.

President Kruger netted about £200,000 for the Exchequer.

At a quarter to five on the evening of June 11th, carts and carriages drew up outside the prison. Barney was one of the first to arrive. Mrs. Phillips, my mother and Miss Rhodes, Frank Rhodes' sister with Mrs. Hays Hammond were all there waiting in their carriages for the prison doors to open.

The four leaders were seen talking to Du Plessis, but none appeared to want to be the first to come out. Du Plessis caught hold of Hays Hammond and jokingly pushed him out into the waiting crowd followed by Rhodes and Phillips. Farrar was the last. They all looked well and with a final handshake with Du Plessis they got into their carriages and drove away. With a shrug of his shoulders Du Plessis closed the gates. His prison could never be the same again.

CHAPTER 5

The Jameson Raid was over, my father was free once more. My mother could not wait to shake the dust of Johannesburg off her feet. All four of the reform leaders packed their trunks and returned to England. Cecil Rhodes was the only one who really suffered. He resigned his premiership of the Cape and went north to Rhodesia to lick his wounds and to continue his dream of the Cape to Cairo railway. 'Does it matter, he said, 'what people say about one, as long as the work goes on'?

Dr Jameson later became Prime Minister of the Cape and a member of the National Convention that framed the Constitution of the Union of South Africa and so it was Dr Jim in the end who helped Rhodes' dream of a united South Africa come true, ten years after he died.

My father left Bedford as a boy, and came back a rich man, far richer than he could ever have expected, even in his wildest dreams and if he had to remain in England for the next few years then the only place to live was near his old home. So my mother and father settled at Chicheley Hall, ten miles from Bedford, and Chicheley became our home in England.

It was a lovely Square Queen Anne house, Built of pink brick. The large hall with its painted ceiling took up most of the centre of the house, with a lovely staircase leading up to the first floor. Most of the bedrooms were on the top floor; approached by a steep narrow staircase, a death trap if the house ever caught fire. All the oak floors were soaked in beeswax and all the main rooms were panelled. One room led into the other room with small powder rooms beyond. We loved Chicheley. It was a wonderful place for children. We called it the lake, but it was really a moat and beyond this lake was a wood called the wilderness where we had a swing. A long hedge separated the terrace from the flower garden. The hedge was so old and so high that it was hollow inside and a wonderful place to hide. There were walled kitchen gardens and a stable yard with loose boxes to hold anything up to 20 horses.

The rooks built their nests in the wilderness and there were ducks on the moat and a pair of swans who usually nested on the fish pond below the lake. The moat was covered with water lilies in the summer. They grew so thickly that the moorhens could run across the lily leaves. Across the field was an avenue of old chestnut trees where the jackdaws nested and a brook where watercress grew and wild forget-me-nots and yellow marigolds. In a spinney nearby we went to pick primroses and pink orchids and, in the autumn to gather hazelnuts. We were woken up in the morning by the quacking of the ducks and the cawing of the rooks. The ducks started on a high note and then came down the scale to a final 'Quack!'. We used to find their nests amongst the reeds in the fishponds, often some way from the water, so they very often survived, but the moorhens who nested under bushes on the moat lost so many of their fledglings because the pike gobbled up the little black puffs of feathers in one mouthful.

We loved Chicheley, there were no hazards. We could walk in the long grass without a care. There were no snakes and scorpions and no mosquitoes at night and above all it was never too hot and the grass was always green.

Our nurseries were right at the end of a long passage on the top floor and all our meals were carried on a tray by the second footman up two flights of stairs and a long passage to the schoolroom. I cannot remember but I do not think the food was very hot by the time it reached the schoolroom.

Just try to eat cold and gluey tapioca pudding! But Nanny said that I must sit there till I ate it and there I sat with a gluey mass on my plate, longing to be outside listening to the ducks and my sisters playing on the lawn and the tapioca by now stone cold and more and more gluey.

But we had much more freedom at Chicheley then we ever had in South Africa. We were able to escape far more easily from the vigilant supervision of Nanny and our governess.

From the very beginning of our lives we were brought up entirely by nurses and governesses. We were in the nursery or in the schoolroom. They punished us, they reprimanded us, and nursed us when we were ill.

My mother was spoilt, she played with us because she was bored, when we were sent back to the nursery.

It was exciting to be with her. Being with my mother and being in the nursery where two different extremes.

After tea we were dressed up in muslin dresses with broad blue satin sashes and sent down stairs. We were so overexcited when we returned to the nursery, dreading our reception by Nanny, that everything always ended in tears. But later on my mother, dressed for dinner, came to kiss us good night.

She blew into the night nursery, the light from the fire gleaming on her evening dress. She lent over our bed with a cheek for each one of us. But you cannot throw your arms round the neck of the Faerie Queene for fear of brushing the tinsel off her wings.

As a boy, my father had saved up his pocket money for a day's hunting, now he filled the stables with hunters and hunted with the Oakley and the Pycheley. I remember once he came back from hunting soaked to the skin because he had swum the river with his horse. He mounted my mother on high-spirited hunters which she had trouble controlling but was undaunted just the same.

From my mother's point of view Chicheley must have been rather close to all my father's relations, even in those days, when it took an hour in a brougham to drive the 10 miles from Chicheley to Bedford. There was my grandmother, and all the Howard's relations, very conscious of the fact that they had given my father his first chance by sending him to South Africa when none of them were prepared to go. There was an Uncle Fred, Headmaster of his school in Bedford, but like all really good men could see through my mother's frivolity to the sterling qualities underneath. All these relations my mother had to contend with.

Then there was her own mother, Granny Waylen, who lived in Paris. She, like my grandmother Farrar, wore black satin dresses, but, unlike my Grandmother Helen, she never looked tidy. She had a mass of grey hair piled on top of her head, but there were always wisps escaping. She had a deep resounding voice and she talked in proverbs. She must have known the book of proverbs by heart and most of Shakespeare. If we quarrelled she would say, 'A house divided against itself cannot stand' in a deep voice. She used to tell us stories about her uncle who was in the Black Hole of Calcutta.

For the rest of her life she lived in London and kept poodles. Every day she took them into Hyde Park and they all sat on chairs and when the park keeper came round she paid for all of them.

My grandmother also told us that her grandmother had lived in India and at the time of the mutiny. She refused to go and hide because she had always been so kind to the Indians that she said they would not harm her. So she stayed in her house and they killed her. But her daughter was taken away and hidden in the swamps and their Indian servants looked after her and brought her food. But she stayed so long crouching in the swamps that she became a hunchback for the rest of her life.

These were the stories that my Grandmother Waylen told us. There was always mystery surrounding my

Grandmother Waylen. She was not down to earth like the Howards. There was something about her. She believed in ghosts. At Chicheley in the nursery was the picture of a spaniel belonging to the owners, the Chesters. This spaniel was reputed to haunt the house. As children we were convinced that we had heard it snuffling underneath our bedroom door and when we had been downstairs after tea, we ran as fast as our legs would carry us back to the nursery. This was the difference between my Grandmother Farrar and our Grandmother Waylen. My Grandmother Farrar would have had no sympathy whatsoever but my Grandmother Waylen would have understood.

Meanwhile, in South Africa, the rift between the Boers and the Uitlanders widened owing to the raid and President Kruger was re-elected president in 1899. "I shall never give them anything." Kruger said, referring to the Uitlanders and throughout South Africa neither race trusted each other and both came to loggerheads on every question relating to legislation of the country, taxation, railways, education and even the official language.

Then in 1899, 20,000 Uitlanders petitioned the Queen for protection. In those days England was the mother country of her colonies and in honour bound to protect her children, the men she had sponsored and encouraged to go out to the outermost parts of her Empire. But the rift between the two races had widened beyond repair and the guns went off almost on their own and in October 1899 the South African War began.

There were three of us now; my sister Helen, myself and Gwendoline, who was born in London in 1897. Even when I was born during the Jameson Raid, my uncle had written to my grandmother, 'It was a great pity it was not a boy'. It was an even greater pity that when my sister Gwendoline arrived it was not a boy either.

Of course, my mother wanted a son, and so did my father and each time yet another girl arrived she must have consoled himself with the thought that next time it was bound to be a boy. She made the best she could out of a bad job.

There was very little difference between the ages of us three, so she dressed us all exactly alike and treated us alike and never referred to us singly but as 'the children'.

We became known as the Farrar children or 'the three disgraces' or 'the three bears' or any other name in the plural. We were never singled out for individual attention, everything we did, we did together. We slept in the same room in identical beds, all in a row we got up and went to bed at the same time, we did our lessons, rode and played together and were never separated. As an entertainment value we were probably quite amusing. If my mother ever referred to us in any other way than as the children it was only when she was annoyed with us and then she called us Helen, Muriel and Gwendoline, all in one breath.

We were not very old before we became aware that one of us ought to have been a boy. It was a disappointment that attached itself to us, not from my father, but from my mother and in a way we vaguely felt that we were a disappointment. She could have loved us more if we had been sons instead of daughters. We were a reminder of a failure on her part, a failure that women are nearly always ascribed to themselves, when they failed to produce the longed for heir. Having failed in this respect she must have been determined to make a feature of us, or possibly a success.

Although she kept us at arm's-length and most of our life was spent in the nursery or the schoolroom, everything was done that could possibly have been done to drill us on a longer-term policy into the semblance of well brought up young ladies. It must have been fairly evident from the start that none of us were likely to become raging beauties. We might have equally never become accomplished, so at least my mother must have hoped that we would be well-behaved, assimilate a certain amount of polish and a few parlour tricks, so a great deal of time in the school room was devoted to deportment. We lay flat on our backs on the floor or on a sounding board. We sat with a weight on our heads. The goal was not really surprising, marriage was almost the only career open to girls in those days. What they termed a brilliant marriage or as second-best, a very suitable one was the culminating success of our education. Large society wedding, every seat crammed and heads craning to get a glimpse of an often tearful bride, was certainly most mothers' dreams. That we might never get married at all or that one day we might want to earn our own livings was never even contemplated.

But I do not think my mother thought as far as that when we were very young. That was to come later, when our growing up pains made us difficult to control and intolerable to have around.

But when we were very young and before we became difficult, she liked to have us asked about. We recited poems, played pieces on the piano and scratched tunes on the violin to entertain her long-suffering guests. We were about six years old when we started our music lessons. Helen and I learned the violin but Gwendoline refused to play anything except the cello.

We owed everything to the two people who taught us at the beginning. Gwendoline was taught by a little man called Kofski. He was either a Russian or Pole and it seems strange that, with his ability to teach, he was eking out an existence in South Africa. His clothes were shabby and he was always hungry. How he lived

I do not know, because he and Mrs. de Kock who taught Helen and I the violin were brought out to the farm twice a week. Mrs. de Kock was equally a wonderful teacher and we learned more from her than we ever did in England or me later on in Germany. They not only taught us to play, but they taught us to love music. They stormed, were temperamental, but also enthusiastic. They drew us out and built us up and we suffered the long hours of practice until the tone deepened and it was no longer just a parlour trick. We discovered music till it flowed into our fingers and into the bow and scratching became a thing of the past. But to Gwendoline the cello became an inseparable part of her life. She had far greater real talent than Helen and I ever achieved.

Miss Berry, our governess, taught us the piano and although she was an experienced pianist herself, she was not much good at teaching. Gwendoline refused to play the piano, anyway not with Miss Berry, but later she played the piano as she played any other instrument she wanted to. It was not long before we were playing trios and quartets with Miss Berry at the piano. She was invaluable to us as an accompanist and to my mother for that matter, because she accompanied my mother's songs; probably one of the reasons why she lasted so long as our governess. She never managed to teach us any lessons. She was far too busy accompanying us all on the piano till the sound of music echoed around the house from morning until night.

If the three of us were taken to a musical entertainment and went to bed like the three bears in identical beds, we would not go to sleep until between us we had pieced together the whole of the show we had seen. If there were any gaps we could not fill in, we pestered our mother to take us again because we simply could not go to sleep until those maddening bits we could not remember had been filled in.

We played musical games in bed, eternally thumped out tunes with our hands on our up raised knees for the other two to guess. If the three of us heard a new tune for the first time, when we went to bed we could piece it together like a crossword puzzle.

'Do you remember, do you remember?' we used to say to each other. It was an irritant those snatches of music until we could consolidate them into a whole and go to sleep.

The first thing I ever remember was lying in the top bunk of the cabin in the Dunvegan Castle. The porthole was shut and every time she rolled green water skewered the light. I was bored and felt sick it was a nightmare. Helen was in the bottom bunk.

My bunk was littered with books, 'Look out, Little Black Sambo! I'm coming to eat you up!' There was a picture of Little Black Sambo in red shorts and a picture of the crocodile with huge teeth and his mouth open wide. It seemed as if I had been lying in the bunk for ages. There was also a book with a picture of Peter Rabbit, in his blue coat and red slippers, but it is Little Black Sambo I remember best. But Mr. McGregor was also trying to catch Peter Rabbit as the crocodile was trying to catch Black Sambo and the sea was trying to catch the Dunvegan Castle. Every now and then I leaned over the bunk and watched my white buckskin boots with white pearl buttons washing backwards and forwards across the cabin floor and every time the ship rolled the water on the cabin floor went swish. No one came near us, the hours turn into days and then at last it was peace, we had arrived at Madeira.

It happened at the beginning of the South African war, the Dunvegan Castle little bigger than a tramp steamer, was loaded to the gunnels with troops going out to the war. She hit the dreaded Bay of Biscay and, having been given up as lost, arrived, with all her boats missing at Madeira a week late, but miraculously she survived the storm and resumed her voyage to arrive safely in Cape Town.

As soon as the South African war was declared, my father returned to South Africa. Five years had passed since the Jameson Road, five years of an uneasy peace. My father, now back, the crowds in London were singing,

Oh God bless you Tommy Atkins,

You're a good'un through and through,

You're a credit to your calling,

And to all your native land;

May your luck be never failing,

May your love be ever true!

God bless you, Tommy Atkins,

Here's your Country's love to you!

The flags were waving, the troops were marching, 'We will soon be back!' they shouted to the waving crowd. Cooks' sons, dukes' sons, sons of millionaires, 40,000 men on foot going to Table Bay, each of them doing his country's work, to look after the things, pass your hat for the country's sake and pay, pay, pay.

The cooks could not follow their sons to Table Bay, but the mothers of the dukes and the millionaires, plus their wives, girlfriends packed themselves onto the overcrowded ships and arrived at the Cape where they got no further or nearer the battle, but helped to console the wounded soldiers.

We also remained at the Cape. My mother took a house called Trovato. I remember the blue periwinkles that covered the ground underneath the trees. Then one day my father gave us each a red leather prayerbook, with our initial stamped in gold and the date across the corner. With the prayer book he gave us a list of hymns we were to learn while he was away at war. Awake my soul and with the sun, fight the good fight, fierce raged the tempest o'er the deep. We knew that one because the ship's band played it every Sunday at sea and the raging tempest had become familiar to us. And then we knelt down beside our beds with him and prayed that he would come back safely and off he went to the war.

My father and his brother Percy took an active part in raising the Imperial light Horse, to the expense of which their firm largely contributed. He became a major on the staff of the colonial division and was one of General Brabant's most trusted guides during the campaign in the Orange Free State and in the Transvaal. He went to the relief of Wepener, where my uncle Percy had got himself besieged. My father had a black pony on which he told us he had ridden 80 miles in one day. The pony was afterwards called Wepener and ended its' days in comfort at Chicheley. We rode him about as children and he could tripple faster than any pony I ever knew. The Boers taught all their ponies to tripple. I imagine the ponies in the Middle Ages ambled, when farmers took their wares to market riding pillion and in Africa where the Boers rode miles in one day, a trippling pony is far less tiring to ride.

The first phase of the war was over at the end of 1900, when General Roberts went home and left Kitchener in charge and that was when the Boers developed guerilla warfare. Their operations continued all through 1901 and into the following year. I imagine that many volunteers like my father and Uncle Percy retired from the fray soon after the first phase of the war was over at the end of 1901. My father was awarded the Queen's medal and the D.S.O. and in 1902 was knighted for his long years of national service.

The first phase of the war had been a British victory in the field and the acquisition of the Transvaal and the Free State. My father went post-haste to Johannesburg to undertake the reorganisation of the goldmines.

The last tragic phase of the war lasted until peace was declared in May 1902.

The Boers fought on in guerilla warfare with exhausted horses, no equipment and very little food. They melted away when they were closely pursued only to rejoin the commandos when the danger was passed.

On March 26th, two months before the end of the war, Cecil Rhodes died in his cottage at the Cape. 'Cecil is very ill.' Frank Rhodes wrote to my father. 'I got the following from Hammerson last night; I should have telegraphed you at once if I thought there was time for you to get here.' But there was not time for my father to return to South Africa, with the end of the South African War and the death within a short time the two great antagonists, Paul Kruger and Cecil Rhodes the history of South Africa changed. But which of the two, I sometimes asked myself, left the most lasting impression on the country they both loved and in what way have they influenced the destinies of the people for whom they fought? Kruger and his Boers or Rhodes and his Rhodesia, or my father and many like him who strove after the war to bridge the gulf between the Boers and the English settlers into a united South Africa?

But one thing is absolutely certain that not one of them ever foresaw very far into the future. Rhodes saw a prosperous South Africa with an increasing white population and a vague idea of equal rights for the natives, but Kruger on the question of native policy was adamant. There was no compromise.

May it be that each one left their imprints on their descendants and that the true native policy in South Africa has not deviated from the time when the Boers and Kruger fought for their existence against the Zulus and Rhodes defeated the Matabele.

To end the war Kitchener took drastic measures on the basis that he had to be cruel to be kind. He destroyed farms, drove off the cattle and the sources from which the commanders received their food were destroyed. The women and children were sent to concentration camps. In my mother's photograph album there is a picture of Eva Baird, very tall. I remember her as a child at the Cape surrounded by Boer wives and children for she, at any rate, was one of the many who had come from England to throng the Cape and did help to alleviate some of the suffering caused by the war. To the bitter end the Boers fought on, sleeping under the stars at night, their clothes in tatters and on the borderline of starvation. The British had mobilised 448,000 men against the Republic's 84,000 and the Boers had kept the British Lion at bay for three years. It was a bitter defeat and a bitter humiliation.

Chamberlain wrote to my father in June 1902,

'I am glad that you share my view as to the terms of surrender finally arranged. We have been generous in regard to money, that we have obtained everything for which we were fighting in regard to policy. I am glad to be assured that Lord Milner will have your hearty co-operation in the heavy work which is now before him. (strangely signed) Yours very faithfully, J Chamberlain.'

While my father was fighting the Boers we were having a wonderful time at the Cape. My mother's house of

Trovato became the home from home for all the wounded officers sent back to base and for a sprinkling of London society who had come out to comfort them. Lady Arthur Grosvenor and Meg who I was always playing pranks with. I remember her dressing up as a Malay for some reason or other. Then there was a Miss Martino who had come out with us on the Dunvegan Castle and had been tied to the leg of the grand piano in the saloon during the storm. Eva Baird, very tall and thin. There is a photograph of her in a group of Boer prisoners, so she at least tried to do something to justify her journey to the Cape.

Amongst the officers who daily thronged Trovato, Sir Matthew Wilson (whose son Peter is head of The Stock Exchange), had an inexhaustible supply of chocolate wrapped in gold and silver paper to represent shillings and sovereigns, which he showered, for us children, over the standard rose trees on the lawns where they fell to earth like golden rain. There was Col Pole Carew who rode with my mother and taught her to stand up on her side saddle like a circus rider. The horse was very quiet but we children were very impressed with her prowess.

And most of all, Lord Basil Blackwood, who illustrated Hilaire Belloc's books and at the time was Deputy Judge Advocate and remained in South Africa until after 1903 when he was assistant secretary to the Orange Free State. He was one of my mother's most devoted admirers.

"What bold hussar or guardsman gay now holds your hand at a play?

Ella, my girl, who watches as you turn away that wandering curl?

Too soon he'll find the course he steers not half so smooth as it appears

Nor free from doubt.

The breeze is fair but quickly veers when you're about.

He thinks you have the sweetest smile

You go on thinking for a while and then, goodbye.

Poor dears, they never know your guile until they try.

My innings anyway is done. I'm out, retired without a run

Clean bowled first ball, pleased to sit by

And watch the fun. Still, hang it all."

They rode, they went with picnics, they climbed Table Mountain and they paddled in the sea at Muizenberg.

It was all great fun. My mother spoilt us and everyone played with us as if we were puppies. They threw us about, rolled us around and sent us to bed when they were tired of us.

But in the nursery we had a nanny we loved. She was the first nanny I ever remember. She had red hair and protruding teeth and no nanny was ever the same to us again. We were terribly upset when she was taken up Table Mountain and chased by the baboons on the way down. When she left us in 1904 we were broken hearted. It was a terrible disaster to lose a nanny that you loved.

Being with my mother was fun, but nanny looked after us when we were ill. She comforted us when we were upset, she understood our every mood and all our problems and she gathered us into her lap and put her arms around us and if we had a nightmare, she was there beside our beds to dispel the bad dreams and smooth out the crumpled sheets and make hot blackcurrant tea when you had a cold and rub your chest with Ellerman's embrocation. The worst thing about being very young was the stifling amount of clothes we had to wear, even in South Africa; thick overcoats and hats, black stockings and boots, a vest, flannel knickers, a flannel petticoat and then the cotton petticoat and a dress, all underneath a coat. It was agony to go for a walk because it was almost impossible to move. We were covered up from head to foot. So was my mother, even her thick skirts were down to the ground and we never saw her except fully dressed, not even in her petticoat and even in bed she was covered up in bed jackets. I can remember her paddling in the sea at Muizenberg, with her long skirts held discreetly just above her ankles, but she never put on a bathing dress and got into the sea. We did, it was the only time we got rid of our clothes.

We had a house at Muizenberg amongst the sand dunes with nothing between us and the thundering surf, white sand and glaring heat, the cold boisterous sea and miles and miles of sand, where nautilus shells sail like fairy yachts through the earth, to come to rest on the shore and seashells of every colour of the rainbow and the great flat sinister jellyfish, so poisonous if you tread on them by mistake. For twenty miles you could ride along the beaches to the other side of the day with nothing except the surf and the sand and the blue of the distant mountains.

We loved to be in the Cape, the sea and the mountains, the bright light and the deep shadows, the silver trees, the leaves as soft and silky as rabbits' ears, the flower girls who lined each side of the street leading from the docks up to the Mount Nelson Hotel, their baskets a blaze of colour with the wild Cape flowers. The gladioli, or the painted ladies as we called them, the Cape heaths and the arum lilies which were so common and the blue disks on the grass like stems and the pig lilies, as they were called, because they grew in such profusion on the Cape flats. On our journeys up to Johannesburg we used to stop the train and get out to pick them.

We travelled in a special coach attached to the back of the train, with its own kitchen, saloon, sleeping berths and an observation car on the back. The journey took three days and two nights.

Once crossing the Karoo desert, we had stopped the train and got out to stretch our legs, but we did not realise, until an hour later that we had left Helen behind. So, the train shunted back for I do not know how many miles until we found Helen, bedraggled and very tearful sitting beside the railway line. Not much fun being left alone in the middle of the Karoo. Gwendoline and I were not sympathetic. We thought it was entirely her own fault.

But later on we were often sent down to the Cape. Johannesburg was not considered a healthy place for the children to stay for more than six months at a time because it was 6,000 feet above sea level and we were supposed to become irritable and highly strung.

If we went, we stayed at Sir Abe Bailey's house in Muizenberg, next door to the cottage which Cecil Rhodes had built and in which he died. It must have been where we were staying at Rust en Vrede that we came to know Rudyard Kipling.

Cecil Rhodes had built him a house not far from Groote Schuur called The Woolsack. It was a one-storey house built around a courtyard with the fountain in the middle and shaded with oak trees. John and Elsie, his two children, were about our ages so we used to go there to play and they used to come and play with us. Mrs Kipling was motherly, fussy and very kind. It was a very happy family without the overlay of nannies and governess. In fact, I do not remember a nanny or a governess.

I just remember Mrs Kipling and John and Elsie and how happy they were together. We were slightly in awe of Mr Kipling. He wore spectacles resting on the end of his nose and he had beetled eyebrows and a bristling moustache. He used to make us to sit in a circle on the grass and he sat cross-legged in the middle, but he never told us stories from the jungle book and read stories from the Arabian nights. We would have preferred the Jungle book. Then, week after week, he assembled us and said, "I will teach you a password which you must never teach to anyone else and which you must always remember no one except Elsie and John and you three children will ever know. It will be your secret code for ever and ever."

And so we sat and laboriously learnt the six words until we were word perfect: Spitzborken, Herborken, Vongrinefaifle, Gobblegoonstadt, Kocksitzen, Kickenveldt, Whiteedorf. This is not the full interpretation because you have to whistle, in one word, click your tongue on another and snort through your nose on the last one. It was extremely difficult to accomplish but all these years have gone past and I have never forgotten it, but it took us ages to learn them perfectly.

We snorted, we whistled and clicked with our tongues. We took it all very seriously. There was nothing light hearted about our lesson. We went on and on until Mr Kipling was satisfied that we have mastered the click, the whistle and the snort in the right places with exactly the right innuendo.

All through these lessons he sat cross-legged glaring at us through his spectacles, unsmiling and dead serious.

I never remember him smiling. It was Mrs Kipling who came to say that tea was ready and with a smile and a flurry broke up our tense circle. He told us that on one of his voyages across the Atlantic the ship had hit a sea monster and the impact was so great that the whole ship shattered. Of course, we believed in sea monsters. We had watched the porpoises following the ship as we crossed the Equator and the flying fish, one of which once landed on our cabin floor through the porthole. And we had stood in the bows of the ship after dark and seen the waves curling away from the prow of the ship alight with phosphorescence like a million fairy lights. And we had gone to sleep to the throb of the engine like the beat of a great heart. And looked for the star of the Southern cross after we crossed the Equator on our way to South Africa and lost them on our way to England as they sank below the horizon. Of course, we believed in sea monsters and in the magic that somehow surrounded all the stories he told us.

It was all part of the beauty of the Cape. We had loved being there during the South African war but the time came when we had to go. The war was over.

My mother took us children back to England at the beginning of 1900 because she was going to have another baby.

So she went into retirement. Her 22- inch waist was expanding and the loss of her figure were something that had to be concealed, almost to be ashamed of, and hidden from public view as much as possible and in July 1900 my sister Marjorie was born at Chicheley. Yet one more daughter. It must have been a bitter disappointment to my mother.

So, we returned to South Africa late in the same year, plus another sister and a new Nanny because our redheaded nanny left us to be replaced by Nanny Elsom, awe inspiring in her starched white dresses and aprons and her large brown eyes which she blinked when she was displeased with us three, which was nearly always.

She adored my new sister Marjorie whom she looked upon as her personal property and fed on milk and slops until she was three years old so that she was constantly being sick. Added to Nanny we now had a governess Miss Berry who was tall and gaunt and thin and brushed her hair over a brown pad which she pinned to her head. She was an accomplished pianist and she also painted. She loved every kind of animal and bird but she did not really like children.

Neither she nor Nanny ever had a day off because there was nowhere for them to go anyway in Johannesburg. She and Nanny remained antagonists all the time they remained with my mother. It was a war that never ceased between the authority of the nursery and the schoolroom and they never in all those years came to terms with each other.

When we arrived back in Johannesburg we children went to live in a separate house to my mother and father but at least we had our ponies as a means of transport, plus our English groom, Pringle. Nearly every house in Johannesburg in those days was a bungalow with the tin roof. So it was quite impossible for us all to get into one house, especially as my mother had her own English staff, a cook, personal maid and my father, a valet.

The whole responsibility of our upbringing was therefore handed over to Nanny Elsom and Miss Berry and we only saw our mother when we rode over with Pringle to visit her. Because Nanny Elsom so obviously preferred Marjorie to us three, we drew closer together and treated our sister Marjorie with contempt. I suppose it was jealousy because it was from Nanny we expected affection. We did not expect affection from Miss Berry. She was in quite another category. And so, for the next three years we lived quite apart from my mother and father, without the normal family life that most children enjoyed even in those days. Although it was the lot of most children to be brought up by nannies and governesses at least they had the consolation that their mothers would come and say good night and even that consolation was denied to us for three long years.

CHAPTER 6

In July 1900 a commission was issued to Lord Roberts to annex the Transvaal and in 1901 with the end of the fighting in sight Lord Milner resigned his governorship of the Cape and arrived in Pretoria to start a civil administration and to reorganise the two new colonies; the Transvaal and the Orange Free State.

In May 1901 the gold mines were allowed to start crushing again. Johannesburg was given a town council and the main body of the Uitlanders were allowed to return to the Rand.

Dated June 5 Chamberlain wrote to my father:

'I am glad that you share my view as to the terms of surrender finally arranged. We have been generous in regard to money, that we have obtained everything for which we were fighting in regard to policy. I am glad to be assured that Lord Milner will have your hearty co-operation in the heavy work which is now before him. Yours very faithfully, J Chamberlain.'

But the second war loan arranged by Mr. Chamberlain was never issued. But the mining houses, headed by my father guaranteed an enormous loan towards the redevelopment of the country.

Education, departments of finance and mines, railways and agriculture were only some of the problems Lord Milner had to face, plus the re-building and re-stocking of the farms for the Boers, who had been dispossessed of their land during the war.

"I mean to have young men to help me," Lord Milner told Sir Percy Fitzpatrick. "I value brains and character more than experience and when I go, I mean to leave behind me young men with plenty of work in them."

Lord Milner offered his young men a wonderful opportunity and a great challenge and responsibility and like all idealists perhaps their sympathies were drawn towards the defeated enemy.

There is no doubt that Kitchener's scorched earth policy was a harsh one, but, on the policy that it would be better to be cruel than to be kind, he must have considered that it was the only way to defeat the guerilla warfare and bring the war to an end.

Perhaps Lord Milner's young men saw eye to eye with Winston Churchill who wrote to Lord Milner in a letter, "The Boers must be helped to rebuild their farms, the gold mines must do that. What more fitting function for the wealth of South Africa? Better to build farms in South Africa than palaces in Park Lane.

Their widows and orphans and crippled soldiers must be our care and once and for all there must be an end of all those ugly stories of bad faith and military dishonour which ten months' experience in the field has convinced me are merely founded on misunderstanding."

And he continues," It must be our policy to run with the hare and hunt with the hounds. I know we have already quarrelled with the Dutch and must not now quarrel with the English. We must be friends with someone."

Somehow Lord Milner's policy had to come to terms with the much maligned mining magnates on the one hand and the Boers on the other. The gold mines were the lifeline of the whole economy of the country and land settlements and agriculture could never prosper on their own in a country that was bereft of water and with poor soil. The wealth of the Transvaal must always live in its mineral wealth and not in its agriculture. One had to be the complement of the other and Lord Milner realised that a prosperous mining industry was the one and only salvation for the Transvaal as a whole. Could he build up the meagre agriculture and the primitive back veldt Boer to be the complement of the highly industrialised gold producing Rand with its English community of businessmen, magnates, engineers and mining experts? Both work miles apart from each other. In one of his speeches he recommended to everyone concerned the promotion of the material prosperity of the country and the treatment of the Dutch and British on absolute equal terms. To reconcile two different races with such wide opposing interests and preoccupations was indeed a gigantic task.

With his land settlement scheme, Lord Milner aimed to increase British agriculture to balance the amount of British in the mining industry. He intended to encourage settlers not only from England but from Canada and New Zealand and he believed that with irrigation more land could be brought into cultivation.

The White River settlement in the Eastern Transvaal was one of his schemes where my sister Helen farms today and where the thriving community grow oranges which are picked and packed on a community system. But it was not until after the 1914 war that White River became fully developed.

Only 12,000 British settlers took advantage of Lord Milner's scheme at the time, nothing like the number of settlers he had hoped for. The main weight of the British continued to be centred on Johannesburg and mining and industry.

There is still some confusion over who were the original members of the Kindergarten. I believe there were only the young men who were chosen by Lord Milner from Oxford University in 1902 who qualified to be known by that name and not the members of his staff, who were with him in the Transvaal before that date. That is Lord Basil Blackwood, John Buchan, Geoffrey Dawson and Herbert Baker the architect. Their names were not included in the term because they were already veterans and trained secretaries on Lord Milner's staff. It was after all a derogatory term applied to the very young and inexperienced by Sir William Mariott, who was practising at the bar in Johannesburg at the time. It was only afterwards when the Kindergarten had proved their ability that that Kindergarten became a word to conjure with, like being a member of a very exclusive club and any young man, however remotely attached to Lord Milner's staff, aspired to have his name linked to the Kindergarten as the highest credential for ability and brains.

Lord Milner and his Kindergarten brought to the Transvaal a graciousness and an intelligence which this raw and undeveloped country had never known. They were young and enthusiastic, with a deep religious sense of the fundamental purpose of life, and entirely divorced from any sense of personal gain.

Whereas the Transvaal in those days was a beehive of industrialists whose main object of remaining in the Transvaal was to make money, the Kindergarten ignored the opportunities for making money that must have come their way. They were only interested in building up the country into an integral part of the Empire. Lord Milner was a great imperialist.

The mining magnates, like my father had battled through the hurly-burly of the early pioneering days and the mining camps and afterwards the misunderstandings and the disaster of the Jameson Raid, were impressed with the ideals of these earnest young men, who saw, in this war rent country, the possibilities of a progressive community with expanding immigration and agriculture and supported by the mineral wealth of the country.

My father, an idealist at heart, but also with the shrewd Christian upbringing by my grandmother, gave Milner his wholehearted support.

Who were the original members of the Kindergarten?

A. S. Amery, who describes himself as informally a member of the Kindergarten says, Geoffrey Dawson, afterwards editor of The Times, Patrick Duncan, afterwards Governor General of South Africa, Lionel Curtis, Lionel Hitchens, chairman of Camell Laird, Fabian Ware, Basil Williams, R. H. Brand and Philip Kerr, afterwards Lord Lothian and John Buchan. But Sir Frederick Jones says, that he included in these names, Dick Feetham, John Dove, Peter Perry, W. F. Moneypenny and Herbert Baker. I believe that the ones who really earned the name were Patrick Duncan, Lionel Curtis, Lionel Hitchens, R. H. Brand, Philip Kerr, Dick Feetham, John Dover and Moneypenny and Peter Parry.

Sometime before my father married my mother, he had bought a farm at about 9 miles from Johannesburg. It was somewhere he could escape from the turmoil of the mining camp and here, through the years, he had planted belts of trees and plantations and an orchard of peach, apricot and cherry trees. The land sloped down from a line of kopjies into a valley where a stream wandered through banks lined with willow trees. At the head of the valley my father built the dam, which irrigated the land in the valley. Here he grew lucerne and crops for his cattle.

On the farm he built a tin bungalow with a living room and three or four bedrooms. The verandah in front of the house was covered with grape vines and climbing roses and there were living quarters for the native servants at the back of the house. The orchard encroached right up to the house, but in front of the garden slipped down to the irrigation stream where roses grew in almost wild profusion.

It was here that, after a short time in our separate house in Johannesburg, we children went to live for the next two years with Nanny Elsden and Miss Berry.

We had our ponies and Pringle our groom, the only reliable means of transport, but for Nanny and Miss Berry who had to endure the discomfort and the hazards of a Cape cart on roads that were nothing more than tracks, the journey into Johannesburg was almost an adventure. Looking back I cannot help feeling sorry for them. We were almost entirely isolated, no telephone, no doctor within 8 miles and no means of communication with the outside world except on horseback or by Cape cart, so naturally they became over anxious about our welfare.

My father used to ride over and spend the weekends with us, but never my mother. But sometimes on Sunday my mother would descend upon us in a fleet of Cape carts with a host of her friends and a wonderful picnic lunch laid out on tables with white tablecloths beneath the shade of the trees. In the cool of the evening they drove away in their Cape carts waving us a laughing goodbye. The farm became a sort of weekend picnic place away from the turmoil of Johannesburg. It was an excuse to go and see how the children were getting on at the cottage. It was just the right distance for a nice ride out into the country. We had other visitors, apart from my mother, in the early morning, one or other of the Kindergarten would arrive and we would ride back with them to breakfast with Lord Milner.

We knew that my mother only came to see us as an excuse for a picnic but we felt that the Lord Milner really wanted to see us when we went to breakfast with him. He had a kind one-sided smile. Except Patrick Duncan, the other members of the Kindergarten, there was no one else for breakfast. We waited in the dining room and after breakfast either Philip Kerr or Patrick Duncan put us on our ponies to ride home.

Once, on my birthday, Philip Kerr gave me a brooch, but Nanny took it away for my sister Marjorie's bib. Lord Lothian would have been 21 at the time with something fey and sad and hair that would simply not stay in the right place. Patrick Duncan's hair on the other hand was cut so short that it was almost cropped and his clothes always seemed too tight for him. Unlike Philip Kerr he was always very tidy. He had beautiful hands, almost feminine and he was so shy that he used to blush. A Scot and a sentimentalist he taught me to read Marcus Aurelius and Robert Louis Stevenson.

'We travelled in the wake of older wars' he read out loud to us.

'And all the world was green

And, love, we found the peace

Where fire and sword had been

They smile and pass, the children of the sword

No more the sword they wield

And yet how green the grass

Along the battlefield.'

But Patrick could laugh, he had a great sense of humour and over the years we got to know him better than any of the other of the Kindergarten. Lionel Hitchens, who afterwards became Chairman of Camell Laird, was a tall, kind, breezy man with a flowing moustache. We were devoted to him because he was so impersonal that he was nice and easy to get on with.

Geoffrey Dawson, who also spent a lot of time at the farm belonged more to my mother's friends than to ours. He was very good-looking with a large brown eyes and Lionel Curtis was easy to get on with because he was so detached that he did not know the ordinary things that were going on around him. I often wonder why they were so kind to us. I am sure they were lonely. There were no young English people of their own age, there were only married people of my mother and father's age and very few people with their intellectual outlook. So they were drawn together in a very close community centred on Lord Milner and his projects.

For us life at the cottage had its ups and downs, we belonged half to Nanny and the nursery and half to Miss Berry and the schoolroom. The cottage was too small to make the classic distinction, but they divided us in half all the same.

It was hard work trying to keep out of trouble with one or other of them because they both had the power to punish us for different crimes against their particular laws.

Gwendoline and I were always in disgrace. Helen did better. She nearly always managed to steer a middle course.

What they termed disobedience was the commonest crime and not speaking the truth, the other. Being late for lessons, being late going to bed, eating too many peaches off the tree or figs or grapes was disobedience.

To tell a man off, my father said to us, do so at once but never ever refer to it again. But unfortunately in the end the strain was too much for Pringle.

Lord Milner's efforts to return the Boers to the land and to rebuild their ruined homesteads and re-stock their farms and to develop the natural resources of the country were hampered by the fact that the gold mines were not producing gold to their full capacity owing to the acute shortage of native labour for the mines. The whole economy of the country, as far as industry and development were concerned, came to a grinding halt as it would today without the natives to supply the manual labour.

So that mining houses asked for leave to import Chinese labourers. Lord Milner reluctantly gave his consent and during 1904 and after, 50,000 Chinese were brought over to the Rand, where they lived in compounds on the mines. My father told us that they each brought with them a handful of Chinese earth to ensure that if they died in South Africa they would be buried in their own soil. They also brought their great delicacies, eggs that had been buried in the ground in black mud for over 50 years. They looked like hard black pebbles.

In respect of the working of the mines and increasing the output plus the revenue, Chinese labour proved to be a complete success. Lord Milner's own object in giving his consent had been not only to put the mining industry on a stable basis, but to restart the colonies on a higher plane than they had ever previously achieved. Chinese labour undoubtedly filled the gap until the economy of the country became stable and until sufficient native labour was recruited to the mines from other parts of Africa, especially Portuguese East Africa. It brought down a storm of protest from the Liberal Party in England, and eventually in 1909 all of the Chinese had returned to their own country, the majority very loath to leave, but by now new mines had been opened, deeper levels had been reached and the mining industry in that Transvaal had become the main gold producing country of the world.

In 1906 when Lord Lothian had become Assistant Secretary to the Intercolonial Council he wrote to my mother: "I really enjoyed staying at Bedford Farm. It has been without question the pleasantest Sunday I have ever passed in South Africa. Feeling refreshed in body, I was still more refreshed through having my artistic tastes, which have grown sadly barren out here, revived. The worst of it is that they now call for more sustenance. A satisfaction that I am afraid I can but seldom offer them, but that is because most people out here have brains and ability but so few accomplishments. Such a state of affairs is the usual accompaniment of a colony but I do not see why it necessarily should be. I only hope other people in Johannesburg will follow the road to Bedford Farm. It would be a much nicer place if they did.'

Whatever impacts Lord Milner and his Kindergarten made on South Africa as a whole, they made an indelible impression on us as children. Lionel Curtis and Lord Lothian stayed until 1909. Patrick Duncan and Dick Feetham remained for the rest of their lives and when Lord Milner left South Africa in 1907 he left behind in a nucleus of young men, as he had predicted, with plenty of work in them and the ability to succeed in the appointed tasks. Before he left South Africa in 1907 Lord Milner said,

"What I should prefer to be remembered by is a tremendous effort subsequent to the war, not only to repair the ravages of that calamity but to restart the colonies on a higher plane of civilisation than they have ever previously attained."

When in 1903 Lord Milner nominated his Legislative Council, my father was one of the first unofficial members to be selected and was the leader of the unofficial members, and the same year he was elected President of the Transvaal Chamber of Mines and it was during his term of office that Chinese labour was introduced to the mines.

From the end of the war and till 1904 he was so busy that we only saw him on very rare occasions; the odd weekend when he came and stayed with us at the farm. He never spoke to us and we did not talk to him either, because he was always so completely absorbed in whatever he was thinking about that he never answered us anyway, but sometimes he had a disconcerting habit of answering a question we had asked him long after we had forgotten what the question had been. But he liked having us with him and we rode for miles, or trotted round the farm after him. He walked so fast that we had to run to keep up, he never seemed to realise that our legs were not long enough to match his stride. But there was always breathing time, when he stopped to look at something, or talk to someone and if we had got too far behind, we caught up during these intervals. Even so, nothing would have persuaded us to stay at home. He was like the Pied Piper with all his children and, wherever he went, we would follow. Sometimes he took us for a picnic into the woods because he loved cooking chops over a wood fire. He said it was the only way to eat chops and we collected the wood and made the fire.

At the farm he always wore grey flannel trousers with leather straps below the knees so that he could ride in them, no collar but a handkerchief tied round his neck and a very old felt hat.

Below the cottage and all along the valley where the land was irrigated by channels from the dam, he employed Portuguese to grow the lucerne and the crops for his cattle. But above the cottage he built farm buildings, cattle pens, and a range of stables and loose boxes for the horses and very nice stone houses for Pringle and his farm managers. He also built us a swimming bath, in amongst the trees. But it was never very successful because there was no chlorination in those days and the leaves fell in and made a scum and there were always frogs. Leading up to the cottage from the dam there was an avenue of mimosa trees and when the mimosa was out in full bloom it was like a cloud of yellow fluff and the scent was almost overpowering. In the spring, when all the fruit blossom was out, the farm looked like those Japanese pictures of peach blossom. Weaver birds built their nests in the willow trees bordering the stream below the cottage. The nests hung from every branch, weighing them down almost into the water. There were so many of them that we could hear the noise of the chattering and they're quarrelling up at the cottage.

Nearly all the plantations my father had planted were eucalyptus trees which are very fast growing, but there were also plantations of scotch fir, so the whole farm was very well wooded and it was like an oasis surrounded by a desert of the high veldt. Everything grew in such profusion provided that there was water that to plant a willow tree it was only necessary to lop a branch off a tree and stick it into the ground and within a year, hey presto, it was a tree.

But there was always the time of reckoning when my father came down to earth and asked Nanny and Miss Berry if they had any complaints to make before he went back to Johannesburg. And of course there always were. So he marshalled us together and gave us a straight talking to and hoped we would do better in the future. We did try, because his talks had far more impact on us than all the punishments that Nanny and Miss Berry meted out.

It was about this time, in 1903, that my father took my mother on an expedition up to Rhodesia to see the Victoria Falls.

In her diary my mother writes,

"My darlings came in from the cottage to see us off." (They were met at Bulawayo by Frank Rhodes who had returned to South Africa after the war and was working in Rhodesia.) They had to trek three days from the railhead in ox wagons and my mother and father rode ponies. My mother says that her side saddle was not very practical because my father's valet, who did the cooking, found it uncomfortable to ride on when my mother was resting in the ox wagon.

At night my mother was afraid of lions, but as they neared the falls and saw the spray rising into the sky and heard the thunder of the water, my mother was so excited that she galloped on ahead so fast that her pony put his foot in a hole and she fell off and her hair and face were covered in dust. The next day she crossed the falls in a blondin by herself, a swing running on a cable across the gorge where the railway bridge was to be constructed. Quite a feat really.

They returned to the railhead and proceeded in their private coach attached to the train to Bulawayo where they drove out to the Matotopos to see Cecil Rhodes' grave. But the trunk she had taken with her evening dresses was stolen from the train, but was later recovered.

My mother does not say in her diary, why she took her evening dresses to the Victoria Falls!

Anyway they arrived back safely and we rode into Johannesburg to welcome them back. Not to our home but to their house.

When they eventually came to see us at the cottage there were naturally more complaints from Miss Berry.

But we had not lived at the farm for much more than a year before my mother decided that the house was too small. So Mr. Baker built on a now much larger dining room with a large room above as a better school room for us. The original dining room Mr. Baker built was a nice family room but my mother wanted a dining room large enough to seat thirty people at least.

Most people in Johannesburg had boys to run the bungalows. Only houses like Government House had English staff. But mother was determined that Bedford Farm was to be properly run so she engaged her staff in England. A butler, two footmen, a housekeeper, her own French maid, our French maid, a laundry maid and two French chefs, not including nanny and Mrs. Berry. In each department they were called boys. In the past they had been warriors not manual workers, but now many of them were hewers of wood and drawers of water for the white people. Whatever they had, at least they had gained peace from the tribal wars which had devastated their villages in the past.

To the white people they were just boys. There were house boys, kitchen boys, pantry boys, garden boys, stable boys or any other kind of boy attached to a particular job. They were never called by their proper names. That was much too difficult. So they were given names by their employers like Jim or James, Charles or John to distinguish one boy from the other. We once had a garden boy who chose his own name. He was called Scissors. They lived in compounds or in quarters behind the house where they were employed. They cooked their own food and when they had made enough money, they went back to their wives and their villages until the money gave out, when they returned to work. They wore white trousers and tunics and went barefoot or wore white sand shoes. Each one was trained by a white member of the staff to do one particular job. One to clean the silver, one to clean the shoes and so on and, provided they were well-trained, they would do that particular job over and over again, exactly as they had been taught without ever deviating. They were supreme copyists and could equally be taught to cook, although they never ate or tasted European food, but they could copy what they had been taught down to a grain of salt with absolute accuracy, so that it was essential to have a highly trained white staff to teach them, with infinite patience. It produced 100% dividend.

We children took them for granted and never learned to speak a word of their language. We spoke to them in a kind of pidgin English which everyone else employed and which they learned to speak and understand, limited to their various jobs. But we did not know where they came from or if they had wives and families or if they were unhappy. I believe they were contented when they were warm and well fed. This applied to the house boys, but the garden boys in the winter often looked terribly cold and absolutely miserable. But when the sun shone they were warm, they laughed together and seemed happy. My mother dressed all the garden boys in dark blue with red berets and I remember her endless discussions with the English gardener about keeping them tidy, otherwise their clothes were deplorable and consisted of cast off European coats or trousers, virtually rags. It was understandable that they could not work wrapped in a blanket, or without clothes as they had been used to in the past, but in the past there had been very few Bantu in the Transvaal. They had come mostly from the coastal regions where the climate was much warmer and the Transvaal during the winter was often very cold especially at night. Even so the problem of clothing them was never considered by most white employers, who, although they clothed their houseboys were prepared to see the garden boys and stable boys going about in rags.

If they were ill I suppose they just lay down and died because there was no one to look after them no hospitals they could go to. But this was 60 years ago and conditions have changed a lot since then. But in those days there were too many problems to be solved too quickly and the welfare of the Bantu was not on the priority list. That problem only came later, when the Chinese went back to their own country and Bantus were imported into the mines from Portuguese East Africa in large numbers to take the place of the Chinese.

It was the enormous influx of native labour into the mines and into the growing industries that produced the problem of their welfare and housing.

On the Farm in those days, it was not native labour but Portuguese from East Africa who grew the crops and looked after the orchards. The Bantu my father employed were either attached to the house and gardens or the stables and they all had their own living quarters. We were hardly aware of them. When we were children they fitted in and were part of the background. We never questioned and there were no wives or piccaninnies as far as I can remember. They were just boys; just Jim who brought up our supper on a tray so quietly in his bare feet that that you never heard him until he was there, milk or soup, he asked. 'Milluck' he would pronounce in a soft drawl or 'souppe' and would put the tray down on the table so softly, so smoothly and smile and then go.

Bedford Farm was a very large house by Johannesburg standards. It was the first attempt on the part of any of the mining magnates to build a house that was home. With the exception of Cecil Rhodes, all the directors of DeBeers diamond mines plus the directors of the goldfields, had absolutely no intention of remaining in South Africa a day longer than was absolutely necessary and they certainly never had any intention of making their homes there. They had come to South Africa to make a fortune and when it was made they were off back to England to live in Park Lane or their own estates in the country plus a string of racehorses. From the diamond fields, the Beits owned a house in Belgrave Square, the Neumanns a house in Piccadilly and Raynham Hall which they leased from Lord Townsend, the Wernhers bought Luton Hoo, but they also owned a house in Piccadilly which is now the Cavalry Club. The Joels had their racehorses, Even Barney Barnato came back. Very few of them remained to plough their money back into the country. It was largely the Jewish community who left, when my father built Bedford Farm he had every intention of making it his permanent home.

It was a challenge, my mother said, to live a civilised life at last and when it was built it was the most beautiful house in the Transvaal.

It was a foregone conclusion that with such a setting my mother soon became the centre of the social and political life of the Transvaal and in Lord Milner's words, 'she gaily imposed a higher plane of civilisation on the colony than it had ever known.' French chefs, butlers and footmen were just a jump ahead of anything Johannesburg society were used to. General Smuts lived in his vine clad bungalow in Pretoria and General Botha lived in his tin bungalow on his farm. But Lady Phillips challenged my mother.

Sir Lionel Phillips, who was Chairman of the Chamber of Mines and one of the four reform leaders, who was sentenced to death with my father, commissioned Mr Baker to build him a house, even larger than Bedford Farm on the outskirts of Johannesburg. All house and very little garden, but it boasted a ballroom which Sir Lionel called the music room because it had a full scale organ on which he played Bach fugues not very well. He was a very small dapper little man, with large protuberant eyes and he always wore a very high collar and a large pearl tie pin (not the sixpenny sort my father wore).

He always seems to have trouble looking over the top of his collar. Lady Phillips was just as small as Sir Lionel and came from Holland. She was fat with tiny feet and hands and a flurry of clothes and words.

The atmosphere of her house was far more intense than the Farm. Lady Phillips knew all about pictures and books which my mother never read anyway and the people who came to the Farm did not go to Lady Phillips' house on pain of death. For instance, John Buchan who was one of Lord Milner's Kindergarten, was a great friend of the Phillips, but never came to the Farm.

So for many years my mother and Lady Phillips kept up a friendly armed neutrality and although they visited each other's houses they did not infringe on each other's guests. But my mother made friendly jokes about them and called Sir Lionel Little Li Phi. I do not know what they called my mother.

CHAPTER 7

Every journey backwards and forwards to South Africa had more or less the same pattern. Three days on the train from the Cape to Johannesburg and 21 days on the boat. The journey from Southampton to the Cape we thought of with trepidation, probably due to the time that we were nearly shipwrecked in the Bay of Biscay. When we crossed Waterloo Bridge on the way to Waterloo station we anxiously looked at the river. If the river was ruffled by the wind we feared the worst and if the river flowed calm and undisturbed our spirits rose. We never had any of these misgivings when we went to board at the Cape on our journey back to England. The Bay of Biscay held no threat on the voyage home, but on the way out it was uppermost in our minds.

I cannot remember ever being seasick, but if it was rough, the first two days out we were forced to remain in our cabins until Nanny or Miss Berry surfaced. My mother, who was a very good sailor, never appeared from her state cabin for the first three days. She waited until the rest of the passengers had found their sea legs and got over their various degrees of seasickness and taken stock of the fellow passengers and then she emerged from her cabin, a radiant picture of health and wellbeing, to dominate the whole ship including the

Captain for the rest of the voyage. Of course she always sat at the Captain's table.

At Cape Town and Southampton there were always a crowd of her friends to see us off and stand on the dock and wave as the ship moved out into the open sea. Her state cabin was always overflowing with flowers and stacks of telegrams wishing her bon voyage and they were all waiting to welcome us home when we docked either at Cape Town or Southampton.

The only variety in each voyage was our fellow passengers. I always remember one voyage when Arthur Somervell, the composer, was on board, every afternoon in the salon he played the piano and my mother sang his songs which he played at a rattling place. "Come into the garden Maud for the black bat night has flown" my mother warbled, as the tempo grew faster and faster and his fingers flew up and down the keys in the running arpeggio accompaniment and his hair stood more and more on end as the excitement grew. "Come into the garden Maud. I am here at the gate alone". Wherever Maud was at the time she could not have missed the fact by the noise that he was making at the gate alone, but we never gathered if she went to meet him because at that moment the steward came to say that they must stop because it was time for tea.

Then there was the Lazy Juggler. He juggled with china plates, throwing them up and catching them, but as the turn went on he began to drop them, too lazy to catch them, he just threw them up and let them fall until he was surrounded by broken china.

On another voyage there was a cowboy. He taught me how to use a lasso and I spent hours practising to swing the lasso over my head. These were the people who fascinated us and we took no time in finding (according to Miss Berry) all the most unsuitable people on the boat. It was left to Miss Berry to try and stop us running wild but she never knew where we were from the first-class passengers to the third class from the boat deck, where my mother and father sat in their deckchairs by special VIP treatment from the Captain, to the engine room. The butchers' shop was one of our particular haunts. We went to see how our cow was getting on and to collect the eggs from the crates of chicken who were there for the sole purpose of laying fresh eggs for breakfast. There were also crates of unhappy cockerels to provide us with roast chicken. On one memorable occasion the butcher wrung the neck of the cockerel for lunch. He left it lying and, when he went back to pick it up, the cockerel jumped up, flapped his wings and crowed, so his life was spared and he became the mascot of HMS Saxon Castle and travelled backwards and forwards across the Atlantic until he died because he never knew when to moult. He was called Bill Bailey.

It must have been on our voyage home in 1904 that General Botha and General Smuts were on board. They were probably going to England to discuss the terms of self government for the Transvaal. There is a snapshot of my father with both of them, all looking very happy together. They were both tall man, General Botha was fatter than General Smuts and he had a short black beard. General Smuts was tall with a fair beard and he was much thinner than General Botha.

A long sea voyage has the effect of bringing all sorts of different people together especially in those days when there was absolutely no communication with the outside world. General Botha and General Smuts were outside our orbit. They were on quite a different plane to the Lazy Juggler and Arthur Somervell. Sir Charles Metcalfe gave us a lot of trouble. He was also tall, but very fat and we did not like him because he decided that we would act scenes from the *School for Scandal* under his tuition. All of which we somehow managed to sidetrack. But there were the children's sports, ship's concerts in which our friend the Lazy Juggler performed and our cowboy demonstrated with his lasso.

Madeira was always the highlight of the voyage. On the outward journey it meant the time when our thick clothes were packed away and the cabin trunks with our summer clothes came out of the hold. They always had a special smell. On the voyage back to England, it was the moment when our summer clothes were packed away and out of the hold came winter clothes, also with a special smell, but this time, mothballs.

There was the expedition up the hill for breakfast and coming down the cobbled streets in baskets on skids. There were beggars with mutilated arms and legs. The baskets and the Madeira embroidery which my mother always bought and with which our petticoats were edged. The precarious journey back to the ship in small boats and climbing up the ladder back onto the deck.

During the last few days of the voyage the temperature changed. People began to draw apart, they became different and when the ship docked and they went on their way with a curt goodbye they were quite different to the people we had known on the voyage. To us it was disillusionment with a big D. The Lazy Juggler had been our bosom friend but he hardly bothered to say goodbye and we never saw him again. We also walked down the gangway into another world. The journey from the farm to Chicheley had taken the best part of four weeks.

It was too far to reach Chicheley in one day from Southampton, so we always stayed the night at Claridges Hotel in London which was our home from home when we were in London. We walked up the stairs to the first floor where my mother had a suite of rooms even for one night.

At Waterloo, we children were put into what was known as a growler, the equivalent of a rather seedy brougham, while my mother and father sailed off in a hansom cab specially hired for the occasion and Hartwell, my father's valet, brought up the rear in a large horse-drawn vehicle with the luggage.

London, how can one go back over so many years? The window boxes in every house in the summer filled with white daisies and red geraniums and the clip clop of the horses' hooves on the wooden block paving, and the straw spread across the street in front of the house where somebody was ill. The guttersnipes who dodged in and out of the horse buses with a shovel, picking up the horse dung and throwing it into bins reserved for the purpose. How is it possible to have lived so many years before there were motorcars, until there are jet planes? To have lived through three wars and to have seen changes, the advent of wireless and television and a landing on the moon, and still to have retained a small semblance of sanity and still to believe that sanity is to be found in the simple things of life; in a lovely day, in the seagulls following the plough, in the thrush and blackbird and the little birds that perish if they are not fed in the winter. The cat who shares our fireside and the dog that barks at the intruder. All the simple things that have always been the same, since long before there were motorcars and jet planes and will continue to be the same long after the first man has landed on the moon.

It was 1904 and we had come from the midsummer into approaching winter. One might have asked why my father chose to take his holiday in England in the winter instead of the summer. The autumn and the winter held the promise of the recreations my father most enjoyed, shooting and hunting and we loved the winter in England away from the perpetual sunshine. Christmas in South Africa in midsummer was never quite the same as seasonable Christmas with possibly snow and sledging and the candles lit on the Christmas tree. Father Christmas seemed much more real in his sledge drawn by reindeers than he did in the middle of summer in South Africa. He must have been so hot.

In the autumn we got up early in the morning and went out hunting and stood outside the coverts while Clarke, our stud groom, who took the place of Pringle when we were in England, cracked hazelnuts for us between his teeth. Nuts did not grow in South Africa and in the garden at Chicheley there was a walnut tree and when the walnuts were ripe we spent hours picking them up. Then the gardeners swept up leaves and made bonfires and the smoke billowed up into the sky on those lovely still autumn days. In the winter there was always a huge log fire burning in the hall and we even had a coal fire in our night nursery, so we went to sleep with the flickering light from the fire casting strange shadows on the ceiling and when it got dark and the curtains were drawn to shut out the night, we would draw the curtains aside and sit with our faces glued to the window pane to watch the first flakes of snow drifting softly down until the ground was white and there was the silence of a muted world.

When Miss Berry insisted on taking us for walks, we bowled our hoops along the road and sometimes we went to children's parties and we drove there in brougham with two horses and a tin hot water bottle at our feet, covered in blue felt. Ten miles was the outside distance to go to parties for the horses and took one hour. I have often wondered how the coachman saw on a dark night as his carriage lamps were lit by two candles. It must have been pretty miserable sitting up on the box on a pouring wet night. We were never allowed to keep the horses waiting. We had to be on the mat when they drew up at the door. They had come out of a hot stable and they got restive if they were kept waiting.

We had our own pony cart that Miss Berry used to drive but one day the pony ran away down Chicheley Hill because she somehow managed to get the reins under its tail, but all was well because it pulled up on the grass verge of the road which were still metal in those days with grass verges, so that riders could canter comfortably along the side of the road and there was hardly any traffic. Chicheley was in the heart of the country, 10 miles from Bedford and 50 miles from London, but already my father was talking of buying a motorcar. But we did have electric light at Chicheley in 1904, driven by a very noisy engine which pounded away all day. But there was no electricity at Lowther Castle in 1922!

My father and his two brothers had an office in London in the City. It had 'Farrar Bros.' written in large letters on the door. My Uncle Sidney, who we hardly knew, was a city businessman and had a home in Stoke Poges and a tall willowy wife who was always delicate.

Uncle Percy was like my father to look at but he was more cautious than my father and did not like taking risks, but he had sound common sense and I imagine often acted as a brake on my father. In South Africa, going back to the early days when they sold the Howard ploughs, the three brothers were a close-knit partnership, but Sidney and Percy hated South Africa and were only too happy to remain in England and run the London office. But Uncle Percy was always ready to dash out to South Africa, as he did during the Jameson Raid, and stand by my father in any emergency. Of the three brothers my father and Uncle Percy were so close together. They both had the same phobia about their feet and they always compared notes about their boots. Uncle Percy's Boots were the most peculiar shape, they curved inwards following the natural shape of his foot and had ventilation holes drilled in the sides. He lived at Brayfield Hall not far from Bedford and he was married to Aunt

Mary who was Scottish and fearless. As an old lady she lived in London during the last war and was completely oblivious of the bombing. She did not know fear and did not understand fear in other people. She was the first woman ever to climb Mont Blanc and it meant no more to her then than going for a walk with her dogs. They had one son, Joey, who had a difficult time between two very positive parents. When Uncle Percy was a boy, my grandmother sent him to school in Switzerland and from that time until he died he only had one real love. Everything else, his wife, Joey, Farrar Bros., all took secondary place. He was a dedicated mountaineer.

When he died at the age of 70, Dr Julius Kugy, a fellow mountaineer wrote of him, 'he was a friend of the mountains and a mountaineer of classical importance and greatness'.

'I believe he liked me as much as I liked him because we only ever wrote or talked about the mountains, leaving aside all personal matters and our everyday life. I have seen English mountaineers at work, I have seen them go off quietly, but steadily, following their game and after completing their mountain trip return unassuming free from any pride. Farrar had all the qualities of a mountain climber, splendidly trained, tough with iron energy and fabulous speed. But what endeared him to us continental climbers were the kindness and understanding for our way of feeling and thinking. He was a valuable link between us and the old Alpine club. He understood everything quickly, readily and entirely and he was just, true and sincere in the interests of the highest mountaineering ideals.

His knowledge of Alpine history was without parallel, moreover, he knew not only all the guides of the last two decades, but their families as well. His knowledge of not only the old guides, but the young ones as well, of all nationalities, was unprecedented, as was also his knowledge and judgment of each one of them. The Bernese Oberland was where he started to climb and the Wetterhorn and the valley Weishorn were the first of the greater Western Alpine peaks that he surmounted. All his life he loved the Oberland and the Wetterhorn, 'He is a very old friend of mine', he used to say, 'and that is why I pay him a visit every year'.'

'The classic beauties of the Bernese Alps had a lasting attraction for him just as the dramatic greatness of the Mont Blanc group had, and close ties bound him to all classes of people.' Dr Julius Kugy goes on to speak about the famous guides, Peter Dangle of Sulden, Kender Bachan who was his guide on the famous second ascent in 1883 of the Weishorn by the west side. 'With one bold leap' the doctor goes on to say 'the young champion reached the middle of the arena and accomplished one of the greatest performances of the time.'

Nine years later Kedanbacken was still his guide and then he speaks of Daniel Maquignas with whom my uncle made the ascent of the Thurnerkamp and the first crossing of the Meoje in 1893.

He was the second to conquer the Peuterey Ridge which he and Maquignas achieved in a storm and they passed a terrible night on Mont Blanc de Courmayeur.

In 1898, the sons of his two guides, Maquinas and Kederbachen junior were his guides at the first ascent of the north of the Wester horn and at the first climbing of a peak named after him, Pointe Farrar, in Aiguille Verte.

From 1901 up till the South African war he was in the Oberland and the Mont Blanc district with and without the guides, amongst other high peaks, but the Bieteschorn and the Matterhorn attracted him and he often spoke with pleasure of the third ascent of its northern end from the east.

The Great War, Dr Kugy goes on to explain sadly, kept him away from the Alps for a number of years, 'But I met him,' he goes on to say, 'on the Anderson Ridge and on many Bernese peaks in 1921 and it must be remembered' he states, 'that at the time he was 64.' In 1921 at the age of 65 he traversed the whole of the Eastern Alps with his favourite guide Daniel, young Camille Maquignas. His last climb was probably the Bifertenstock in 1928 at the age of 70.

He became most known as well for his writings as perhaps as a mountaineer which he wrote equally fluently in French and in German. 'Farrar's works,' Dr Kugy says, 'are not overloaded with feeling and cheap philosophy but they are the outcome of genuine sentiment. The Anglo Saxon is only seldom understood by the Continental in this respect. Farrar unearthed the guidebooks of famous pathfinders and his notes and essays are a treasure trove of Alpine knowledge. His help in all Alpine matters was unequalled.

He was always ready to help young mountaineers with advice. He helped with the equipping of the first Everest expedition in which his special authority was invaluable.

He was Vice President of the Alpine club and editor of the Alpine Journal from 1909 to 1926, And in Canada, another mountain is named after him, Mount Farrar, in the Rocky Mountains

'There are unbreakable ties between mountaineers.' he wrote to Dr Kugy and he had been an active mountaineer for nearly 50 years. No wonder he wrote to my grandmother from Johannesburg at the time of the Jameson Raid, 'I cannot wait to get back to my beloved mountains.'.

It was Uncle Percy who always met us at Southampton whenever we returned to England. It was he who looked after Chicheley when my father was in South Africa and managed the farm and the shooting and saw that the stables were full of high-class hunters for my father's return with three ponies for us and the donkey with a pannier for my sister Marjorie.

But it was my grandmother who engaged the staff and supervised the house so that when we walked into Chicheley everything was ready for us, down to the smallest detail.

But for Helen, Gwendoline and me, it was my cousin Joey we looked forward to seeing more than anyone else. He was like an older brother and he, being an only child, and we, having no brothers, we probably each supplied the companionship that we all lacked. And although he was 10 years older than us he was never too old to make us feel too young.

Riding home from hunting one day through Bedford he said, 'Look, children, how nice we all look in the shop windows.'

Once during the winter he fished Helen out of the river when she slipped off the bridge below Brayfield and carried her up to the house wrapped in his coat.

He was always kind, not only kind to us, but to everyone and especially animals. The only time I ever remember him being cross was when he saw a man hit a dog out shooting. He would not tolerate any form of cruelty or injustice.

His inseparable companion was a white fox terrier with a black patch over one eye called Molly, but one day when he was about 16 he took Molly out rabbit shooting and shot her by mistake and we wept for Molly and we wept for Joey because he could not forgive himself for killing Molly who he loved so much.

George and Marjorie in foreground and
Ella and Muriel in the background

CHAPTER 8

To my father 1905 was a vital year. Although it had been agreed at the time that the Chinese would return to their own country, after the time their agreement has expired. The Boers, all the same, feared that the Chinese would remain and the same problems would arise in the Transvaal that had arisen in Natal with a large Italian population who, in the past, had been brought into the country to work the sugar plantations and had remained and increased and had raised an insoluble problem, accepted by neither white nor Bantu.

So the Boers rose in protest against the importation of Chinese labour to the mines.

General Botha came out of his retirement on his farm and with the help of General Smuts took on the leadership of the Het Volk Party, recently formed by the Afrikaners in the Transvaal whose objects were to press for responsible government.

They were an ideal partnership, General Smuts providing the brains and drive and Botha the solid personal side, in contact with all types of people. Together they decided to devote all their efforts to the rebuilding of a united South African nation.

But the Boers were not united, General Hertzog in the Orange River Colony had the following of the diehard Boers, whose slogan 'Africa for the Afrikaners', bitter and unreasoning, was to grow in the years to come and cause a rift in the efforts of the English and the Het Volk to form a united country out of British and Dutch alike.

The Liberal Party, who hated Chamberlain, Lord Milner and all their works, saw an opportunity for using Chinese labour as an electioneering weapon against Chamberlain. So General Botha and General Smuts found firm allies in the Liberal Party in England. Alfred Lyttleton, who was secretary for the Colonies at the time had agreed that Lord Milner's work for the reconstruction of the colonies had so far progressed, that steps should soon be given to give the Transvaal representative government.

So when my father introduced Chinese labour to the mines he threw a rock into the area of political world which had far reaching repercussions. It roused the Boers out of their defeated retirement and in England it helped to bring the Liberals into power in the election of 1904. Lord Milner was overruled by Campbell Bannerman and the Liberal Party and it gave the Transvaal responsible government in 1906.

'They gave us back our country,' Smuts said, 'in everything but name. Only people like the English could do it. They may make mistakes but they are big people.' Lord Milner retired and he came out to the Farm to say goodbye to us. In the eight years of his administration, he said, before he left the country, he laid deep and strong the foundation upon which a united South Africa would become one of the great states of the Empire and further he said, 'what I should prefer to be remembered by is a tremendous effort, subsequent to the war, not only to repair the ravages of that calamity but to start the colonies on a higher plain of civilisation then they have ever previously attained.'

And so he left and many people like my father must have wondered what the future of the country would be. As Leader of the Progressive party my father plunged into politics to prepare the way for the first general elections to be held in 1907. The burning political problems became the main topics of conversation at the Farm and Helen, Gwendoline and I were old enough to understand and become almost as partisan as the most diehard amongst my father's friends.

We listened and absorbed politics from morning to night because we were always with grown people when we were not in the schoolroom. The vital issues were far more important to us than any of the lessons Miss Berry tried so hard to teach us. From living at the cottage our world had suddenly expanded and we were swept up into the orbit of dynamic personalities and unbounding enthusiasm and energy. There was never a dull moment, except when we had to do our lessons and never a dull person amongst my father's friends and so the Farm became the political centre for the English and the Progressive party.

My mother's Sunday lunches became an institution when 20 to 30 people sat down in the new dining room and all the afternoon guests poured out to the Farm. But at lunch provision was always made for the uninvited, a relic of the old pioneering days when no one was ever refused hospitality and so they came riding, or in Cape carts, the invited and the uninvited, every Sunday and my mother made them all welcome. However many people, we three always had our lunch in the dining room. We sat on high chairs and when we were not eating, we sat with our hands behind our backs. If we sagged, my mother noticed it at once, 'Children' we heard from the end of the table, 'sit up straight and put your hands behind your backs.' It was not often that she had to tell us. It was too embarrassing to be told off in front of a room full of people so we took care to avoid being reprimanded.

In the afternoon my mother sat on the stoep and entertained those guests who were only too pleased to spend a lazy afternoon sitting around in comfortable armchairs. But my father played endless games of golf croquet on the lawn in front of the house and often we three were sent off to take some of the guests down to the farm to see the cattle. On a hot afternoon, after a large lunch, it was a grind we did not always enjoy; all the way down the gardens and the climb back up the hill in the heat.

And always there was a background of political discussions. Everyone talked a lot about burying hatchets and forgetting the past that the British and the Boers were as far apart as they had ever been. I cannot remember either General Smuts or General Botha ever coming out to the Farm, or any other Boers for that matter and never their wives. We never met either Mrs. Botha or Mrs. Smuts and I am sure that my mother never met them either. But my mother always told us that Mrs. Smuts cooked General Smuts' lunch with a Greek book in one hand while she stirred the pudding with the other hand.

The Boers lived in their own watertight compartments and as far as I can remember there was never any social contact between the races. A great deal of the talk about burying a hatchet was mostly on the surface. We children looked upon Hertzog as a terrible ogre and we were more English than the English and more anti-Boer than the most extremist elements. As children we probably emphasised the extremes in all we heard to make it more realistic in our understanding. And so the struggle for political supremacy started in 1905 to culminate in the elections of 1907.

Lord Selbourne succeeded Lord Milner in 1905. He was quite different, or so we thought as children. Lord Selbourne often carried a walking stick, we particularly noticed this because no one had a walking stick in South Africa because they never walked, they rode everywhere. He wore jaunty white Panama hats, which were not really like him. He had a very pleasant speaking voice and a happy friendly smile. He was not at all awe inspiring, but shy and difficult to talk to. I would think that he got on well with everyone but had very few close friends and he was completely unbiased and never took sides. I would think at first the English-speaking people were disappointed that he was so non-committal and did not champion their cause as Lord Milner had done. But he gained the confidence and the respect of the Boers and the friendship of General Smuts as Lord Milner had never been able to do.

Lady Selbourne, who was Lord Salisbury's sister and endowed with all the brains of the Cecils, was way above our orbit and I think she found it difficult to talk to children and equally difficult to talk to the wives of the rich Johannesburg businessmen, because she was devoid of small talk and was probably more at home with the wives of the Boer farmers when she could talk with knowledge about their homes and their children.

I think she liked my mother because my mother was always surrounded with so many people that it was not possible to have any kind of conversation. But my father was a great admirer of Lady Selbourne and he talked easily to her as we never heard him talk to any other woman. He never went into a brown study in the middle of lunch when Lady Selbourne was there, as he did with people who bored him. She always kept his interest.

Her youngest son, Luly Palmer, was with them for a time in South Africa, before he went to school in England and was about our age. Like most small boys he hated washing and we were slightly curious when we were continuously being made to wash that neither Lord or Lady Selbourne ever told him to wash his hands, so he often came to lunch with hands filthy. Once he waded into my mother's lily pond and came into lunch smelling of mud, having dried off in the sun, without changing. We would have got into terrible trouble and been punished by Nanny if it had been one of us, so we held our breath to hear what would happen, but nobody said a word and I do believe that neither Lord for Lady Selbourne even noticed.

Lady Mabel Palmer was much older than Luly, she was about 20, not pretty but attractive and like many intelligent people she never bothered about her clothes and her hair was untidy and I do not think that Lady Selbourne noticed this either, which we did not understand because she was always so tidy herself.

There were so few unmarried girls that age amongst the English people who came to the Farm and, as very little about people escaped our notice, we soon discovered a budding romance between Lady Mabel and Charlie Howick, afterwards Lord Grey.

This is the first time romance had come our way at the Farm and we were fascinated, so we conspired to bring them together on the crowded Sunday afternoons and sidetrack the other people who wanted to talk to them and, unbeknown to them, we made ourselves into a sort of bodyguard at the weekends. Then, one memorable Sunday afternoon, all our efforts were rewarded. We managed to cover their retreat as they escaped up the hill behind the Farm. When they returned and announced that they were engaged to be married we felt it was entirely due to our good staff work!

My impression is that the Selbournes were not only a happy family, but two people who lived the principles they believed in without any sense of superiority or bias and quite unconsciously.

They filled a very difficult position at a very difficult time and did more to bridge the gulf between the English and the Boers than anyone else could possibly have done. Simply by their impartial and friendly attitude to English and Dutch alike, by their example of unassuming, intelligent people.

CHAPTER 9

Helen was 10, I was nine and Gwendoline was 8 years old when we returned to South Africa in 1905.

Our tearful goodbyes had been said to Joey and all our Chicheley friends. For the next seven years, more often than I can remember, we waved goodbye from the decks of the Union Castle steamers as the band played Auld Lang Syne and hawsers splashed into the water and we slowly moved away into the open sea.

There were too many changes, too many heartbreaks and too many goodbyes. No wonder we were difficult children.

But like all children we lived in the present and the past was soon forgotten. We lived every moment of the voyage, and made lifelong friends we never saw again once the ship had docked. We drew near to the Cape our excitement grew. Who would be waiting for us on the docks? What new excitements were in store for us when we got back to Johannesburg?

Mr. Baker had completed Bedford Farm while we had been away. We all moved into the new house before the paint was barely dry and our life at the cottage with Nanny and Miss Berry was over.

Although it was called Bedford Farm, the house had very little resemblance to the farmhouse. It had about 25 rooms and a pillared stoep, a tradition of all South African houses and like Groote Schuur it was a copy of the old Dutch house with White Gables and a terracotta tiled roof.

Simplicity, my mother has decided was the keynote to a farmhouse, so in England she had collected Sheraton and Chippendale furniture, and a few Dutch landscapes to hang on the walls. The bathrooms were lined with old Dutch tiles she had collected in the same way from old curiosity shops in Bedford and all over the country. But the dining room table and chairs were made out of South African stink wood by local craftsmen. The floors and the main staircase were made of polished oak and instead of carpets my mother collected Persian rugs. The beds came from Maples or Heals in London, so my mother combined simplicity with every modern comfort.

Then Helen had a romance. It was the first of many that we were to follow each other in rapid succession. I always knew which young man was in favour. Our yardstick was the English poets. To one she read Longfellow to another Tennyson and so on. It was Swinburne and she wanted to marry him. But my mother said: 'No'.

POSTSCRIPT

The young man for whom Helen chose Swinburne as wooing material may well have been the red haired Australian Basil Hobson whom she did eventually marry and who was father of her 3 children. He was a relative of Valerie Hobson, the actress and film star, who was married to Jack Profumo, who was Minister of War at the time of his ill fated liaison with Christine Keeler. She stood by him and assisted in his redemption by working alongside him for a charity in the East End of London.

Sadly, the memoir is discontinued at this point. Most was written in the late 1950s when she was about 60. She was living on her own at Thwaite Hill Farm, overlooking Ullswater. Like her father she was a chain smoker. She was not good at looking after herself, often not eating for long periods. I remember staying with her around this time and seeing her working on memoir. She does not mention the pensione to which she was sent in Germany shortly before the outbreak of The First World war when she was about 15. I have seen letters written to her there by her father. Her mother did approve of her marriage to Anthony Lowther because she went to stay with them shortly after they were married. They had 3 children but the marriage did not last. She had 11 grandchildren to some of whom she was close but she lived a pretty spartan existence in her latter years at Thwaite Hill Farm after an early life in luxurious surrounds. She devised and ran a small charity called 'Evergreens', which enabled elderly people to visit parts of The Lake District in a Minibus guided by Muriel. As her memoir depicts, she was a shrewd observer of all goings on around her as a child and her account is far more compelling than mine because it is first hand evidence. I have tidied up a few little typing mistakes and grammatical errors but no more.

Andrew Watson